At Sylvan, we believe that everyone can master math skills, and we are glad you have chosen our resources to help your children experience the joy of mathematics as they build crucial reasoning skills. We know that time spent reinforcing lessons learned in school will contribute to understanding and mastery.

Success in math requires more than just memorizing basic facts and algorithms; it also requires children to make connections between the real world and math concepts in order to solve problems. Successful problem solvers will be ready for the challenges of mathematics as they advance to more complex topics and encounter new problems both in school and at home.

We use a research-based, step-by-step process in teaching math at Sylvan that includes thought-provoking math problems and activities. As students increase their success as problem solvers, they become more confident. With increasing confidence, students build even more success. The design of the Sylvan workbooks lays out a roadmap for mathematical learning that is designed to lead your child to success in school. Let us partner with you to support the development of confident, well-prepared, independent learners.

The Sylvan Team

Sylvan Learning Center
Unleash your child's potential here

No matter how big or small the academic challenge, every child has the ability to learn. But sometimes children need help making it happen. Sylvan believes every child has the potential to do great things. And we know better than anyone else how to tap into that academic potential so that a child's future really is full of possibilities. Sylvan Learning Center is the place where your child can build and master the learning skills needed to succeed and unlock the potential you know is there.

The proven, personalized approach of our in-center programs deliver unparalleled results that other supplemental education services simply can't match. Your child's achievements will be seen not only in test scores and report cards but outside the classroom as well. And when he starts achieving his full potential, everyone will know it. You will see a new level of confidence come through in everything he does and every interaction he has.

How can Sylvan's personalized in-center approach help your child unleash his potential?

• Starting with our exclusive Sylvan Skills Assessment®, we pinpoint your child's exact academic needs.

• Then we develop a customized learning plan designed to achieve your child's academic goals.

• Through our method of skill mastery, your child will not only learn and master every skill in his personalized plan, he will be truly motivated and inspired to achieve his full potential.

To get started, simply contact your local Sylvan Learning Center to set up an appointment. And to learn more about Sylvan and our innovative in-center programs, call 1-800-EDUCATE or visit www. SylvanLearning.com. *With over 850 locations in North America, there is a Sylvan Learning Center near you!*

3rd Grade
Jumbo Math Success
Workbook

Published in the United States by Random House, Inc., New York, and in Canada by Random House of Canada Limited, Toronto.

This book was previously published with the title *3rd Grade Super Math Success* as a trade paperback by Sylvan Learning, Inc., an imprint of Penguin Random House LLC, in 2010.

www.sylvanlearning.com

Created by Smarterville Productions LLC
Producer & Editorial Direction: The Linguistic Edge
Producer: TJ Trochlil McGreevy
Writer: Amy Kraft
Cover and Interior Illustrations: Shawn Finley, Tim Goldman, and Duendes del Sur
Layout and Art Direction: SunDried Penguin
Director of Product Development: Russell Ginns

First Edition

ISBN: 978-0-375-43051-0

This book is available at special discounts for bulk purchases for sales promotions or premiums. For more information, write to Special Markets/Premium Sales, 1745 Broadway, MD 6-2, New York, New York 10019 or e-mail specialmarkets@randomhouse.com.

PRINTED IN THE UNITED STATES

20 19 18

Basic Math Success Contents

Basic Math Success Contents

Math Games & Puzzles Contents

Math Games & Puzzles Contents

Math in Action Contents

Math in Action Contents

3rd Grade
Basic Math Success

Lunch Boxes

WRITE the total number of food items you see in the four lunch boxes.

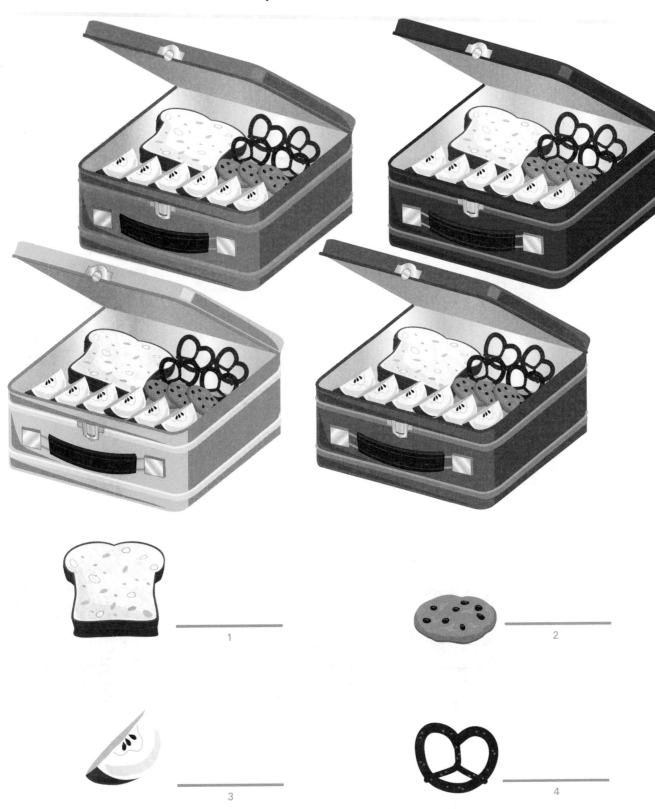

1. _____

2. _____

3. _____

4. _____

Pick a Package

How many of each type of box would be needed to pack the chocolates on the conveyor belt?
WRITE the answer below each box.

1

2

3

4

Get in Line

SKIP COUNT and WRITE the missing numbers.

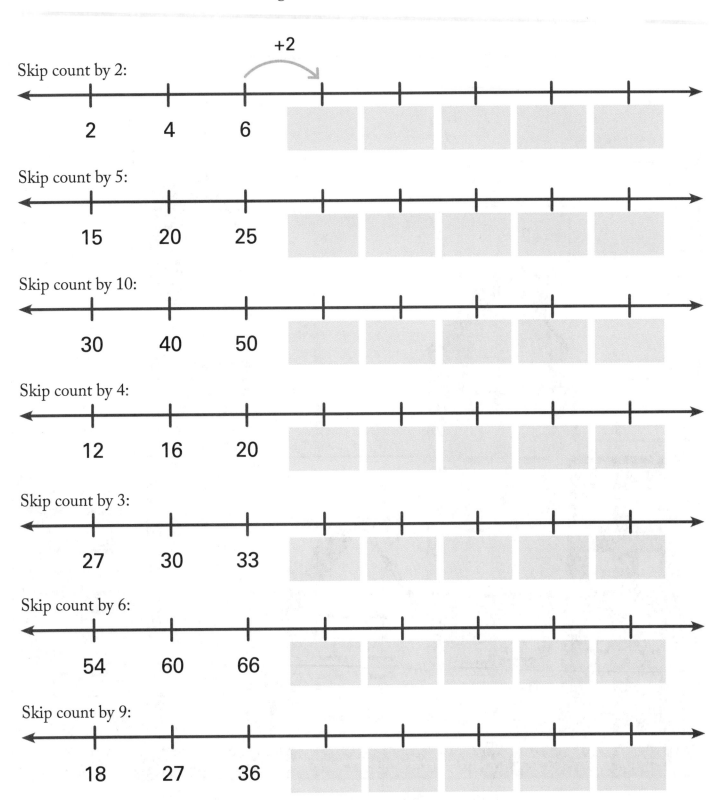

Skip count by 2:

+2

2   4   6

Skip count by 5:

15   20   25

Skip count by 10:

30   40   50

Skip count by 4:

12   16   20

Skip count by 3:

27   30   33

Skip count by 6:

54   60   66

Skip count by 9:

18   27   36

Buildings Times Two

WRITE the number of windows you see on each building on the sign above the building.

Picture It

Use the pictures to help you answer each problem. WRITE the answer for each set of pictures.

$5 \times 3 =$ _____
₁

$9 \times 3 =$ _____
₂

$7 \times 3 =$ _____
₃

$6 \times 4 =$ _____
₄

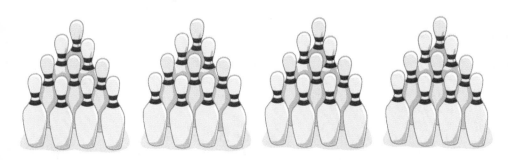

$10 \times 4 =$ _____
₅

High Fives

Use the pictures to help you answer each problem. WRITE the answer to each problem.

HINT: Think of each problem as counting the total number of fingers on a number of hands.

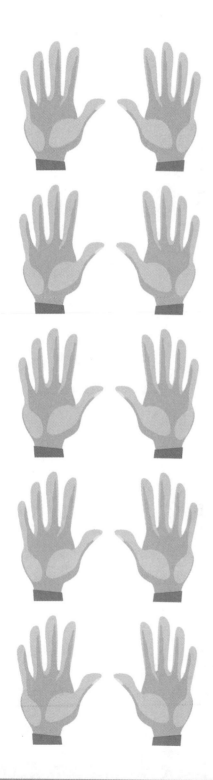

$4 \times 5 =$ ___20___

1

$1 \times 5 =$ _____

2

$7 \times 5 =$ _____

3

$6 \times 5 =$ _____

4

$2 \times 5 =$ _____

5

$9 \times 5 =$ _____

6

$5 \times 5 =$ _____

7

$8 \times 5 =$ _____

8

$10 \times 5 =$ _____

9

$3 \times 5 =$ _____

10

Magic Tricks

Multiplying any number by 1 gives you the same number.

Each hat has 1 rabbit.
3 hats have 3 rabbits.
3 × 1 = 3

Multiplying any number by 0 gives you 0.

Each hat has 0 rabbits.
3 hats have 0 rabbits.
3 × 0 = 0

WRITE the answer to each problem.

1.	2.	3.	4.	5.	6.
6 × 1	7 × 0	3 × 1	2 × 0	10 × 1	8 × 0

7.	8.	9.	10.	11.	12.
5 × 1	4 × 0	1 × 1	5 × 0	9 × 1	10 × 0

13.	14.	15.	16.	17.	18.
7 × 1	6 × 0	8 × 1	1 × 0	2 × 1	9 × 0

Picture It

Use the pictures to help you answer each problem. WRITE the answer for each set of pictures.

1.

$7 \times 4 =$ _____

2.

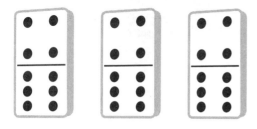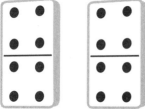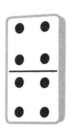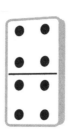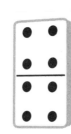

$10 \times 3 =$ _____

3.

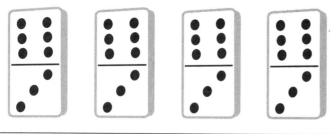

$8 \times 6 =$ _____

4.

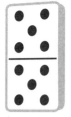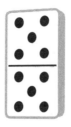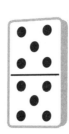

$9 \times 4 =$ _____

5.

$10 \times 6 =$ _____

Computation Station

A **product** is the number you get when you multiply two numbers together. A **factor** is one of the numbers being multiplied.

Example:
6 factor
× 7 factor
4 2 product

factor →

×	0	1	2	3	4	5	6	7	8	9	10
0	0	0	0	0	0	0	0	0	0	0	0
1	0	1	2	3	4	5	6	7	8	9	10
2	0	2	4	6	8	10	12	14	16	18	20
3	0	3	6	9	12	15	18	21	24	27	30
4	0	4	8	12	16	20	24	28	32	36	40
5	0	5	10	15	20	25	30	35	40	45	50
6	0	6	12	18	24	30	36	42	48	54	60
7	0	7	14	21	28	35	42	49	56	63	70
8	0	8	16	24	32	40	48	56	64	72	80
9	0	9	18	27	36	45	54	63	72	81	90
10	0	10	20	30	40	50	60	70	80	90	100

LOCATE each factor in the multiplication table. The square where the row and column meet shows you the product. WRITE each product.

1. 2 × 5
2. 8 × 4
3. 10 × 10
4. 3 × 9
5. 5 × 7
6. 6 × 1

7. 10 × 3
8. 0 × 7
9. 4 × 3
10. 7 × 7
11. 9 × 6
12. 5 × 5

13. 8 × 2
14. 4 × 9
15. 3 × 7
16. 9 × 0
17. 8 × 8
18. 2 × 1

Multiplying

Computation Station

WRITE each product.

1. $4 \times 1 =$ _____
2. $7 \times 5 =$ _____
3. $8 \times 3 =$ _____

4. $6 \times 2 =$ _____
5. $9 \times 5 =$ _____
6. $10 \times 2 =$ _____

7. $6 \times 6 =$ _____
8. $1 \times 0 =$ _____
9. $1 \times 8 =$ _____

10. $9 \times 9 =$ _____
11. $7 \times 4 =$ _____
12. $5 \times 3 =$ _____

13.
$$\begin{array}{r} 10 \\ \times\ 8 \\ \hline \end{array}$$

14.
$$\begin{array}{r} 0 \\ \times\ 2 \\ \hline \end{array}$$

15.
$$\begin{array}{r} 9 \\ \times\ 4 \\ \hline \end{array}$$

16.
$$\begin{array}{r} 5 \\ \times\ 6 \\ \hline \end{array}$$

17.
$$\begin{array}{r} 8 \\ \times\ 2 \\ \hline \end{array}$$

18.
$$\begin{array}{r} 4 \\ \times\ 4 \\ \hline \end{array}$$

19.
$$\begin{array}{r} 7 \\ \times\ 3 \\ \hline \end{array}$$

20.
$$\begin{array}{r} 9 \\ \times\ 8 \\ \hline \end{array}$$

21.
$$\begin{array}{r} 4 \\ \times\ 2 \\ \hline \end{array}$$

22.
$$\begin{array}{r} 1 \\ \times\ 1 \\ \hline \end{array}$$

23.
$$\begin{array}{r} 6 \\ \times\ 3 \\ \hline \end{array}$$

24.
$$\begin{array}{r} 9 \\ \times\ 5 \\ \hline \end{array}$$

25.
$$\begin{array}{r} 4 \\ \times\ 5 \\ \hline \end{array}$$

26.
$$\begin{array}{r} 10 \\ \times\ 4 \\ \hline \end{array}$$

27.
$$\begin{array}{r} 0 \\ \times\ 0 \\ \hline \end{array}$$

28.
$$\begin{array}{r} 2 \\ \times\ 9 \\ \hline \end{array}$$

29.
$$\begin{array}{r} 5 \\ \times 10 \\ \hline \end{array}$$

30.
$$\begin{array}{r} 3 \\ \times\ 3 \\ \hline \end{array}$$

Fair Share

The twins aren't happy unless they get the same number of everything. How many of each toy will they each get? WRITE the answers.

1. _____ cars

2. _____ marbles

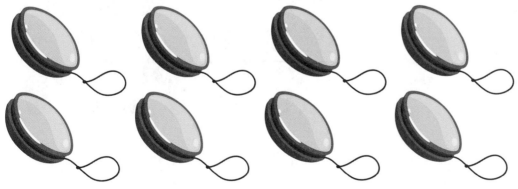

3. _____ yo-yos

Fair Share

WRITE the number of gems each pirate will get if they split the treasure equally.

1 _____

2 _____

3 _____

4 _____

Bugged Out

CIRCLE groups of three bugs. WRITE the number of groups in each set.

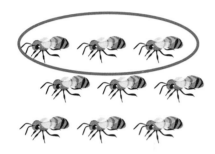

9 ÷ 3 = _____
1

15 ÷ 3 = _____
2

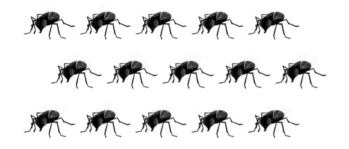

27 ÷ 3 = _____
3

18 ÷ 3 = _____
4

Iced Over

Use the pictures to help you answer each problem. WRITE the answers.

HINT: Count the number of ice cubes in each group.

$18 \div 3 =$ _____
₁

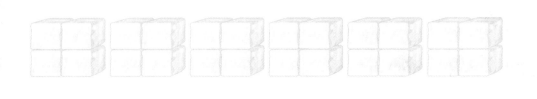

$24 \div 6 =$ _____
₂

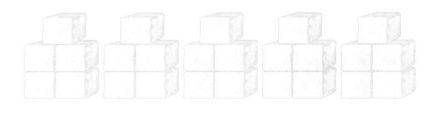

$25 \div 5 =$ _____
₃

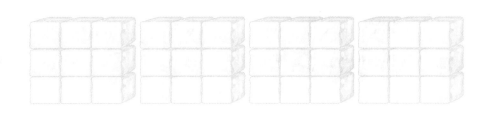

$36 \div 4 =$ _____
₄

$20 \div 10 =$ _____
₅

Computation Station

A **quotient** is the number you get when you divide one number by another number. You divide the **dividend** by the **divisor**.

Example:

```
       6    quotient
divisor 3 ) 18  dividend
```

×	0	1	2	3	4	5	6	7	8	9	10
0	0	0	0	0	0	0	0	0	0	0	0
1	0	1	2	3	4	5	6	7	8	9	10
2	0	2	4	6	8	10	12	14	16	18	20
3	0	3	6	9	12	15	18	21	24	27	30
4	0	4	8	12	16	20	24	28	32	36	40
5	0	5	10	15	20	25	30	35	40	45	50
6	0	6	12	18	24	30	36	42	48	54	60
7	0	7	14	21	28	35	42	49	56	63	70
8	0	8	16	24	32	40	48	56	64	72	80
9	0	9	18	27	36	45	54	63	72	81	90
10	0	10	20	30	40	50	60	70	80	90	100

WRITE each quotient.

1. $2 \overline{)\, 16}$
2. $8 \overline{)\, 24}$
3. $9 \overline{)\, 90}$
4. $1 \overline{)\, 7}$
5. $3 \overline{)\, 21}$
6. $7 \overline{)\, 14}$

7. $5 \overline{)\, 35}$
8. $7 \overline{)\, 56}$
9. $4 \overline{)\, 32}$
10. $8 \overline{)\, 48}$
11. $9 \overline{)\, 81}$
12. $2 \overline{)\, 12}$

13. $7 \overline{)\, 63}$
14. $1 \overline{)\, 3}$
15. $10 \overline{)\, 70}$
16. $3 \overline{)\, 9}$
17. $9 \overline{)\, 36}$
18. $4 \overline{)\, 40}$

Dividing

Computation Station

WRITE each quotient.

1. $20 \div 5 =$ _____

2. $80 \div 8 =$ _____

3. $12 \div 6 =$ _____

4. $18 \div 2 =$ _____

5. $24 \div 3 =$ _____

6. $30 \div 6 =$ _____

7. $90 \div 10 =$ _____

8. $56 \div 8 =$ _____

9. $36 \div 6 =$ _____

10. $45 \div 5 =$ _____

11. $16 \div 4 =$ _____

12. $3 \div 1 =$ _____

13. $5 \overline{)15}$

14. $5 \overline{)25}$

15. $6 \overline{)24}$

16. $10 \overline{)60}$

17. $9 \overline{)72}$

18. $1 \overline{)8}$

19. $2 \overline{)6}$

20. $4 \overline{)40}$

21. $7 \overline{)63}$

22. $4 \overline{)28}$

23. $3 \overline{)27}$

24. $7 \overline{)49}$

25. $6 \overline{)54}$

26. $7 \overline{)14}$

27. $3 \overline{)30}$

28. $9 \overline{)45}$

29. $6 \overline{)48}$

30. $5 \overline{)20}$

Factor Hunt

WRITE all of the factors of each number. Use the multiplication table to help you.

HINT: Write down all of the numbers that can be used to divide each number evenly. Remember that every number can be divided by itself and 1.

Example:

10   1   2   5   10

×	0	1	2	3	4	5	6	7	8	9	10
0	0	0	0	0	0	0	0	0	0	0	0
1	0	1	2	3	4	5	6	7	8	9	10
2	0	2	4	6	8	10	12	14	16	18	20
3	0	3	6	9	12	15	18	21	24	27	30
4	0	4	8	12	16	20	24	28	32	36	40
5	0	5	10	15	20	25	30	35	40	45	50
6	0	6	12	18	24	30	36	42	48	54	60
7	0	7	14	21	28	35	42	49	56	63	70
8	0	8	16	24	32	40	48	56	64	72	80
9	0	9	18	27	36	45	54	63	72	81	90
10	0	10	20	30	40	50	60	70	80	90	100

1. 4

2. 6

3. 9

4. 12

5. 15

6. 16

7. 18

Tic-Tac-Toe

A **multiple** is a number that can be divided evenly by another number. CIRCLE any number that is a multiple of the blue number. PUT an X through any number that is not a multiple. DRAW a line when you find three multiples in a row. The line can go across, down, or diagonally.

Example:

5

42	10	24
16	35	40
25	5	81

5

X̶4̶2̶	⑩	X̶2̶4̶
X̶1̶6̶	㉟	㊵
㉕	⑤	X̶8̶1̶

Multiples of 5 are
5, 10, 15, 20, 25,
30, 35, 40, 45, 50.

2

12	18	16
4	7	9
3	15	20

10

55	20	49
70	36	72
50	80	30

6

40	14	12
25	54	36
63	8	18

8

56	36	24
27	80	64
48	34	30

Any Way You Slice It

WRITE the fraction for each picture.

Example:

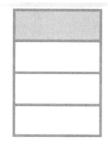

$\dfrac{1}{4}$ ← the number of shaded sections
← the total number of sections

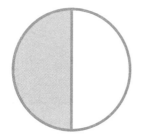

_____
1

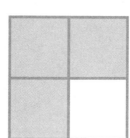

_____
2

_____
3

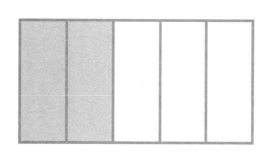

_____
4

_____
5

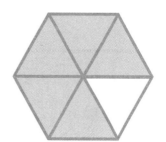

_____
6

Piece of Cake

COLOR the cake pieces to match each fraction.

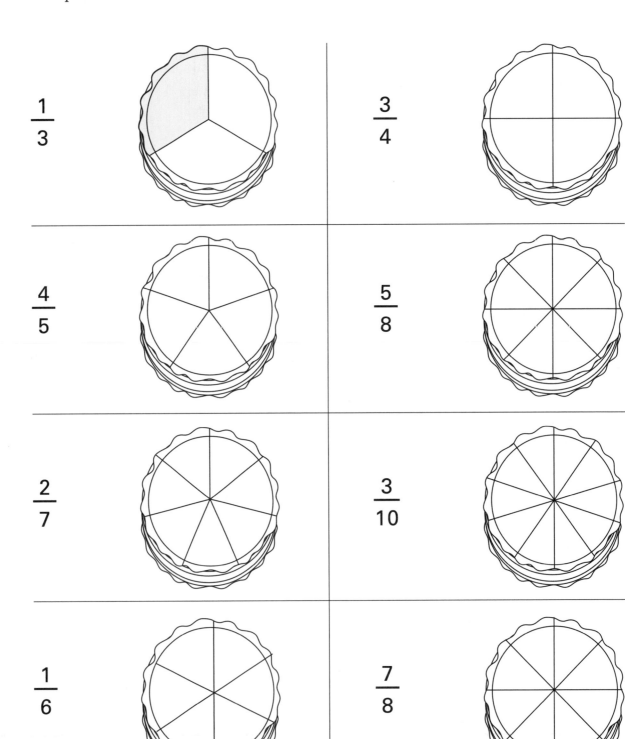

Fraction Bars

WRITE the fraction for each picture.

_____
1

_____
2

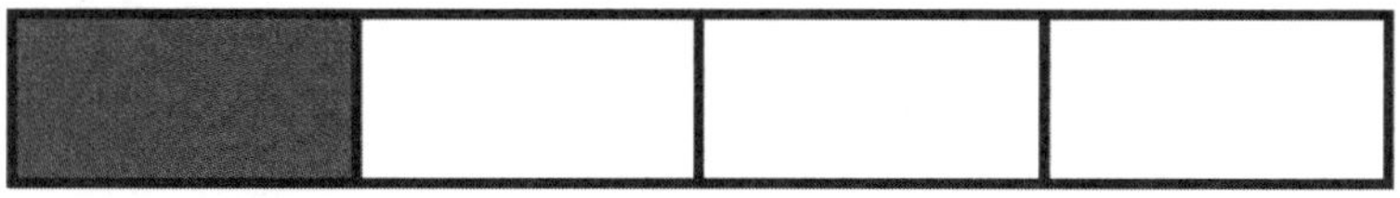

_____
3

_____
4

_____
5

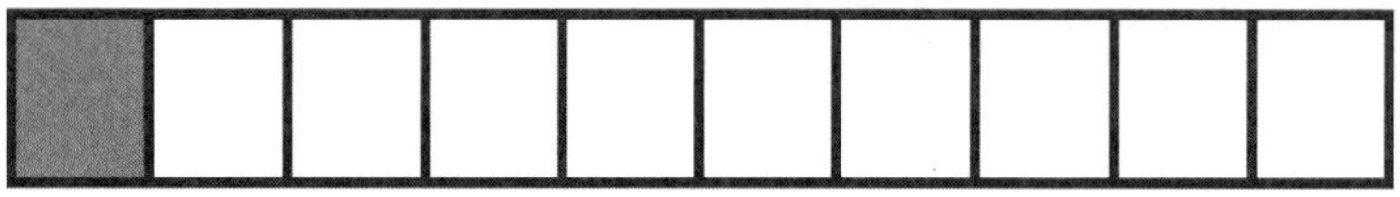

_____
6

_____
7

_____
8

Odd One Out

CROSS OUT the picture or fraction in each row that does **not** match the others.

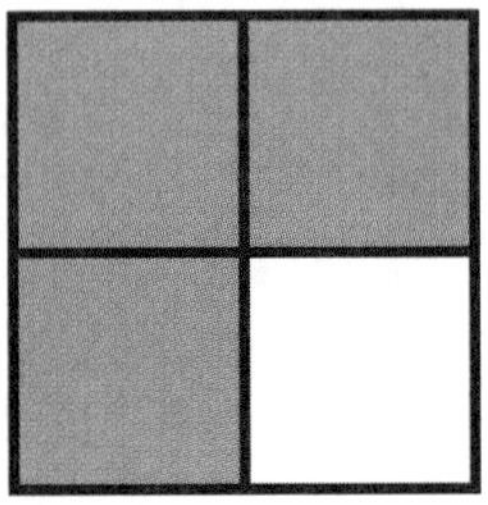

$\frac{3}{4}$

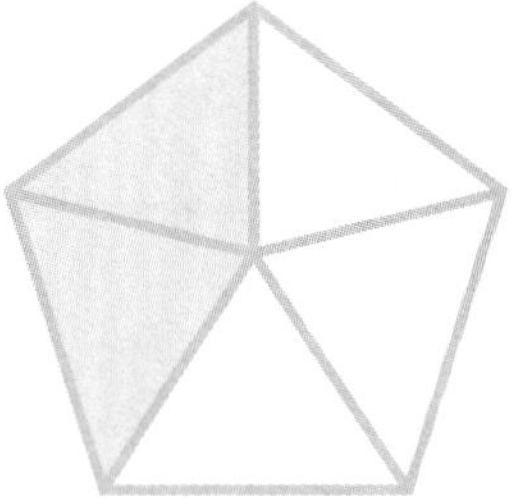

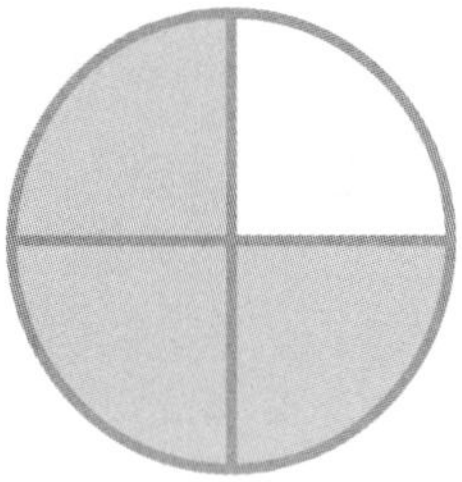

$\frac{5}{6}$

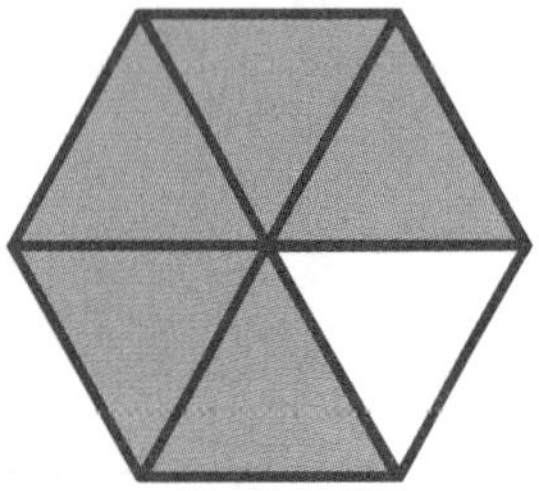

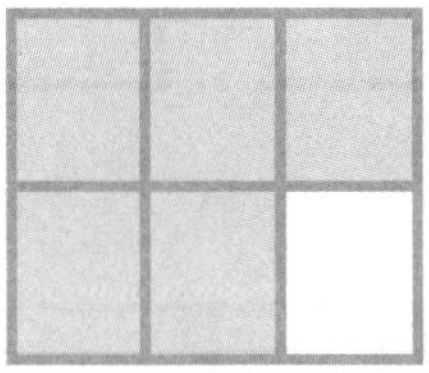

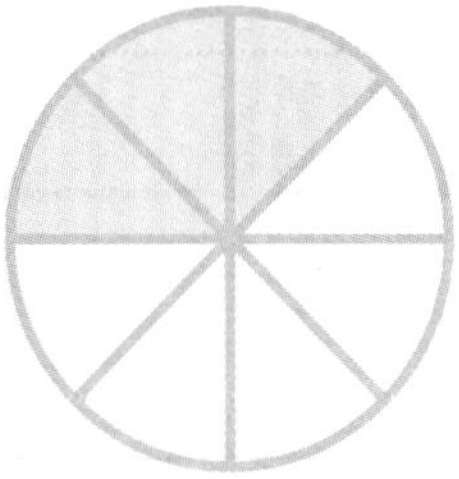

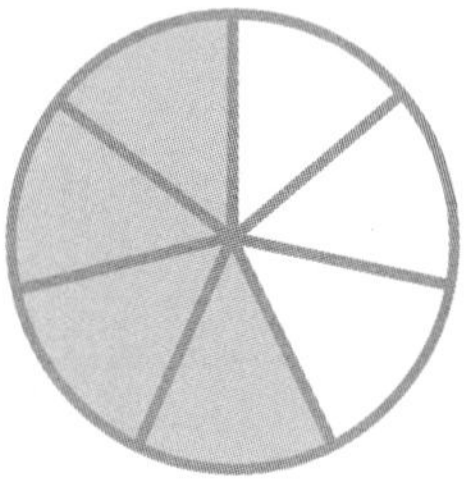

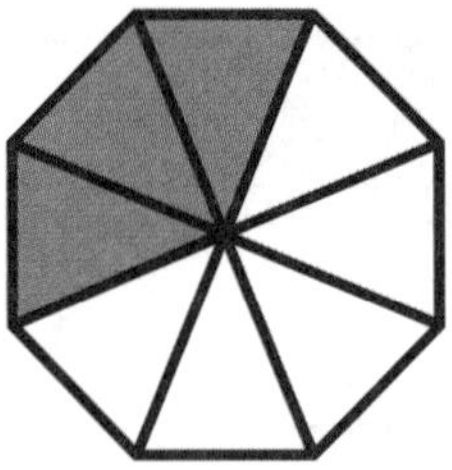

$\frac{3}{8}$

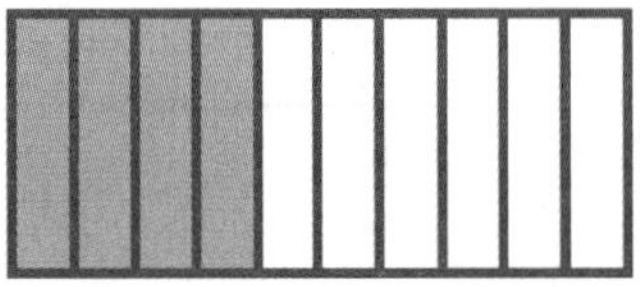

$\frac{4}{9}$

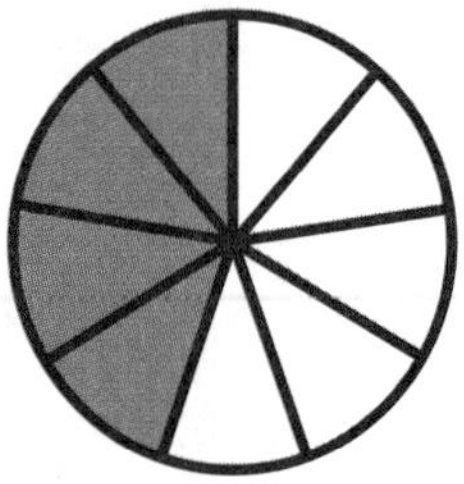

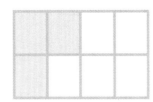

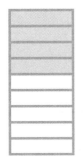

Shaded Shapes

WRITE the fraction for each set.

Example: $\dfrac{5}{6}$ ← the number of shaded circles
← the total number of circles

_____ 1

_____ 2

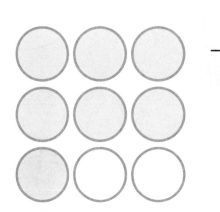

_____ 3

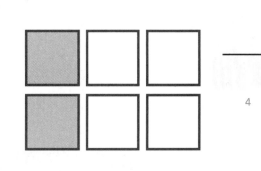

_____ 4

_____ 5

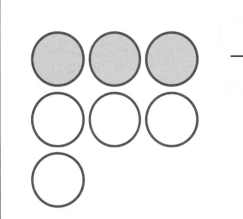

_____ 6

Jellybean Jars

COLOR each jar of jellybeans.

$\dfrac{3}{7}$ green

$\dfrac{4}{7}$ blue

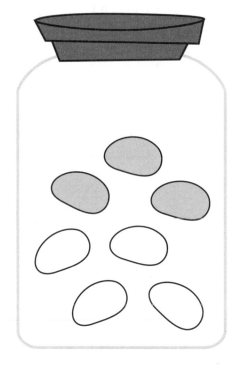

$\dfrac{1}{8}$ purple

$\dfrac{2}{8}$ green

$\dfrac{5}{8}$ orange

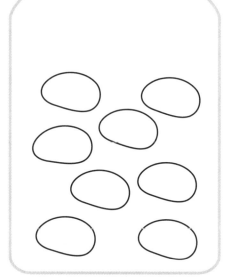

$\dfrac{2}{10}$ red

$\dfrac{3}{10}$ yellow

$\dfrac{5}{10}$ purple

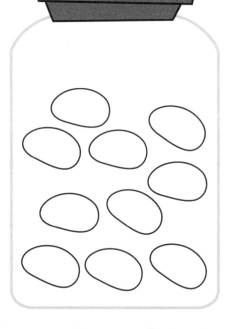

$\dfrac{1}{9}$ orange

$\dfrac{2}{9}$ red

$\dfrac{3}{9}$ blue

$\dfrac{3}{9}$ purple

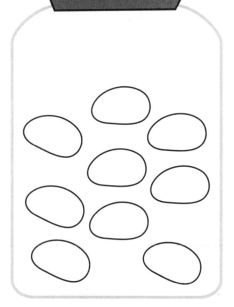

Fashion Fractions

WRITE the fraction for each description.

1. Fraction of kids wearing orange shirts $\dfrac{3}{7}$

2. Fraction of kids wearing hats —————

3. Fraction of girls wearing skirts —————

4. Fraction of boys wearing sunglasses —————

5. Fraction of girls with red hair —————

6. Fraction of boys wearing shorts —————

Find the Same

CIRCLE the picture in each row that matches the fraction.

$\dfrac{4}{5}$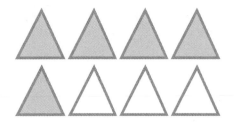

$\dfrac{7}{9}$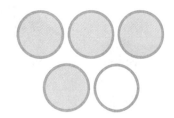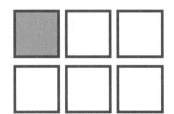

$\dfrac{1}{6}$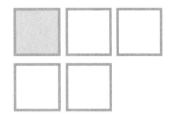

$\dfrac{3}{10}$

Piece of Cake

COLOR the cake pieces to match each fraction. Then CIRCLE the larger fraction.

HINT: The larger fraction is the one with more cake colored.

$\dfrac{1}{6}$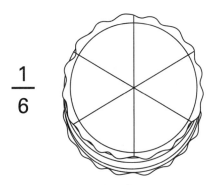

$\dfrac{1}{5}$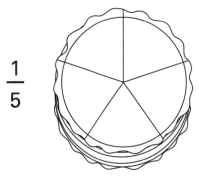

$\dfrac{4}{7}$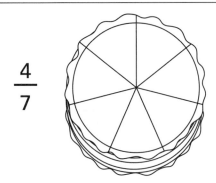

$\dfrac{3}{8}$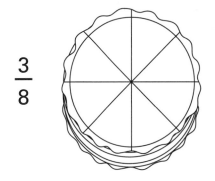

$\dfrac{1}{4}$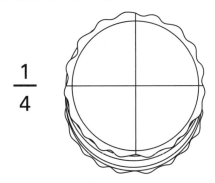

$\dfrac{2}{9}$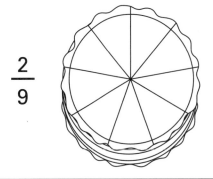

$\dfrac{7}{10}$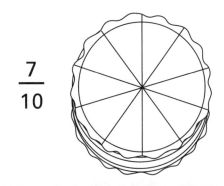

$\dfrac{7}{8}$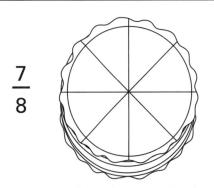

Matched or Mismatched?

WRITE >, <, or = in each box.

HINT: Use the fraction bars to help you picture the fractions.

$\dfrac{1}{3}$

$\dfrac{1}{4}$

$\dfrac{1}{5}$

$\dfrac{1}{6}$

$\dfrac{1}{7}$

$\dfrac{1}{8}$

$\dfrac{1}{9}$

$\dfrac{1}{10}$

$\dfrac{2}{5}$ ☐ $\dfrac{1}{4}$
1

$\dfrac{5}{6}$ ☐ $\dfrac{1}{3}$
2

$\dfrac{1}{6}$ ☐ $\dfrac{4}{9}$
3

$\dfrac{4}{8}$ ☐ $\dfrac{5}{10}$
4

$\dfrac{7}{10}$ ☐ $\dfrac{7}{8}$
5

$\dfrac{4}{4}$ ☐ $\dfrac{5}{8}$
6

$\dfrac{5}{9}$ ☐ $\dfrac{6}{9}$
7

$\dfrac{2}{7}$ ☐ $\dfrac{2}{4}$
8

$\dfrac{5}{9}$ ☐ $\dfrac{4}{10}$
9

$\dfrac{3}{6}$ ☐ $\dfrac{3}{7}$
10

$\dfrac{5}{7}$ ☐ $\dfrac{5}{8}$
11

$\dfrac{7}{7}$ ☐ $\dfrac{9}{9}$
12

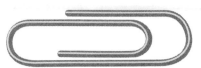
Measure Up

WRITE the approximate length of each object in inches (in.) and centimeters (cm).

1. about _____ in.   about _____ cm

2. about _____ in.   about _____ cm

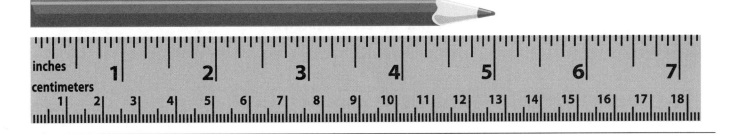

3. about _____ in.   about _____ cm

4. about _____ in.   about _____ cm

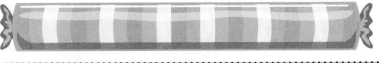

Rulers Rule

MEASURE each piece of ribbon with a ruler. WRITE the approximate length of each object in inches (in.) and centimeters (cm).

1.

about _____ in.   about _____ cm

2.

about _____ in.   about _____ cm

3.

about _____ in.   about _____ cm

4.

about _____ in.   about _____ cm

5.

about _____ in.   about _____ cm

6.

about _____ in.   about _____ cm

Preferred Measure

Which unit of measure would you use to measure each object? CIRCLE *inch*, *foot*, or *yard*.

NOTE: These rulers show how the units compare to each other. They are not actual size.

inch

foot

yard

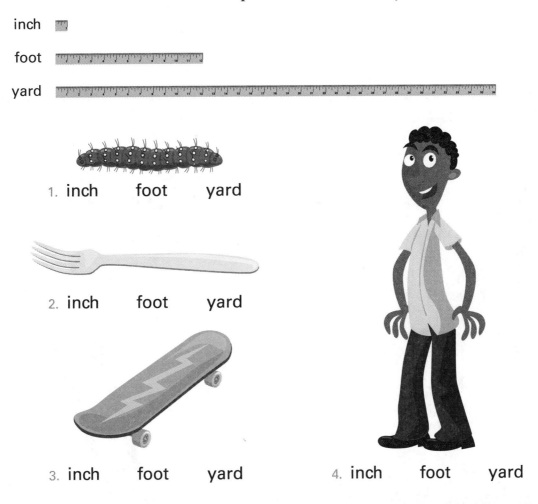

1. inch   foot   yard

2. inch   foot   yard

3. inch   foot   yard

4. inch   foot   yard

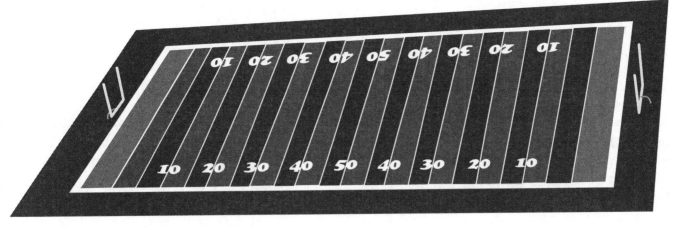

5. inch   foot   yard

Length

Which Is Best?

Which is the best unit to measure the length of each object? CIRCLE *centimeter* or *meter*.

NOTE: These rulers show how the units compare to each other. They are not actual size.

centimeter

meter

1. centimeter   meter

2. centimeter   meter

4. centimeter   meter

3. centimeter   meter

5. centimeter   meter

6. centimeter   meter

Match Up

DRAW lines to match the pictures with equal amounts of liquid volume.

Example:

2 cups = 1 pint   2 pints = 1 quart   4 quarts = 1 gallon

Liquid Volume

Which Is Best?

Which is the best unit to measure the liquid volume of each object? CIRCLE *cup*, *pint*, *quart*, or *gallon*.

1. cup   pint   quart   gallon

2. cup   pint   quart   gallon

3. cup   pint   quart   gallon

4. cup   pint   quart   gallon

5. cup   pint   quart   gallon

6. cup   pint   quart   gallon

7. cup   pint   quart   gallon

8. cup   pint   quart   gallon

Circle the Same

CIRCLE any item that can hold at least 1 liter of liquid.

Example:

1 liter (1 L)
1 liter = 1,000 milliliters

120 milliliters (120 mL)

Which Is Best?

Which is the best unit to measure the liquid volume of each object? CIRCLE *milliliter* or *liter*.

1.   milliliter   liter

2.   milliliter   liter

3.   milliliter   liter

4.   milliliter   liter

5.   milliliter   liter

6.   milliliter   liter

7.   milliliter   liter

8.   milliliter   liter

Circle It

CIRCLE any item that weighs less than 1 pound.

Example:

1 pound (1 lb)
1 pound = 16 ounces

1 ounce (1 oz)

Which Is Best?

Which is the best unit to measure the weight of each object? CIRCLE *ounce* or *pound*.

1.   ounce   pound

2.   ounce   pound

3.   ounce   pound

4.   ounce   pound

5.   ounce   pound

6.   ounce   pound

7.   ounce   pound

8.   ounce   pound

Circle It

CIRCLE any item that weighs more than 1 kilogram.

Example:

1 kilogram (1 kg)   1 gram (1 g)
1 kilogram = 1,000 grams

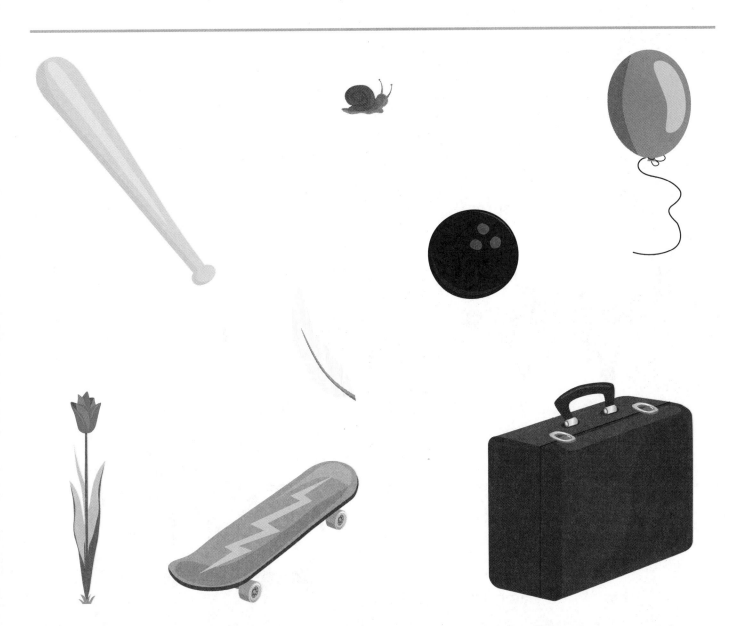

Which Is Best?

Which is the best unit to measure the weight of each object? CIRCLE *gram* or *kilogram*.

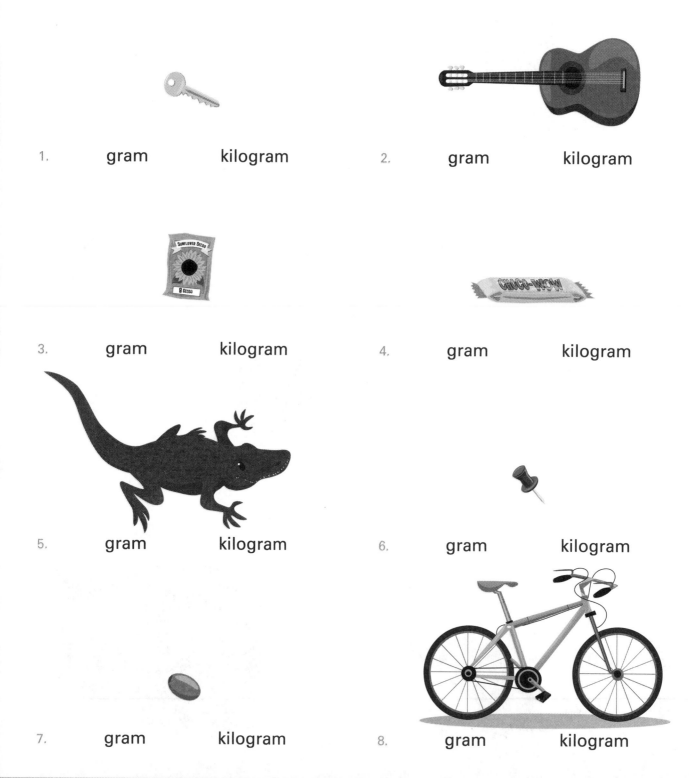

1.   gram   kilogram

2.   gram   kilogram

3.   gram   kilogram

4.   gram   kilogram

5.   gram   kilogram

6.   gram   kilogram

7.   gram   kilogram

8.   gram   kilogram

Measure Up

MEASURE each temperature to the nearest degree. WRITE the temperature in degrees Fahrenheit (°F) and degrees Celsius (°C).

Example:

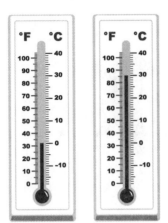

Water freezes at 32°F or 0°C.
A hot summer day might be 86°F or 30°C.

1. _____ °F

_____ °C

2. _____ °F

_____ °C

3. _____ °F

_____ °C

4. _____ °F

_____ °C

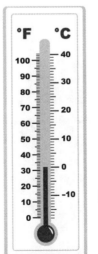

5. _____ °F

_____ °C

6. _____ °F

_____ °C

Circle It

CIRCLE the appropriate item of clothing for the weather shown on each thermometer.

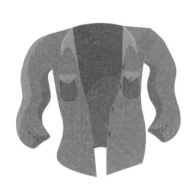

Matched Set

COLOR all of the shapes in each row that match the word.

HINT: A square is a special type of rectangle.

circle

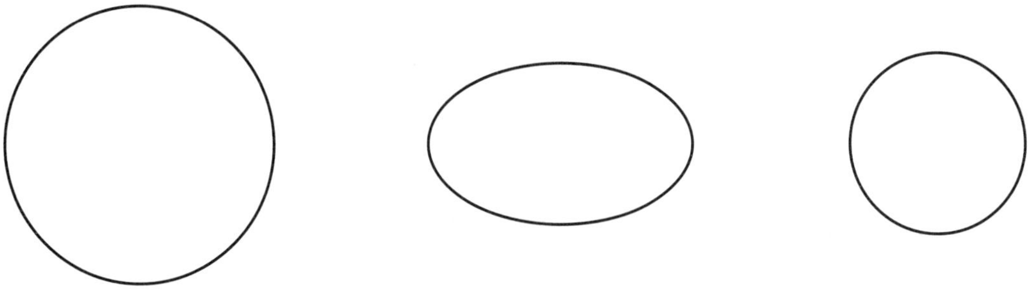

square

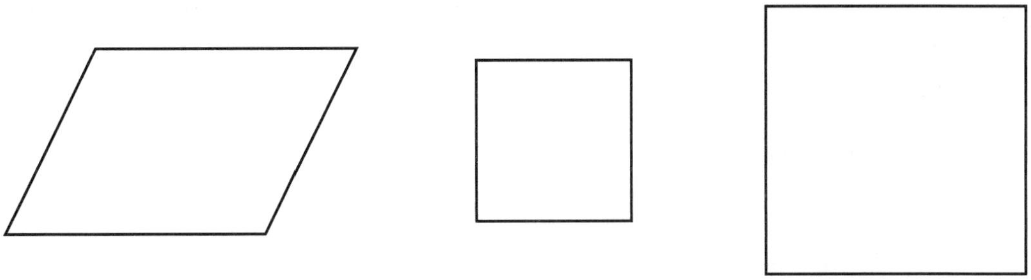

triangle

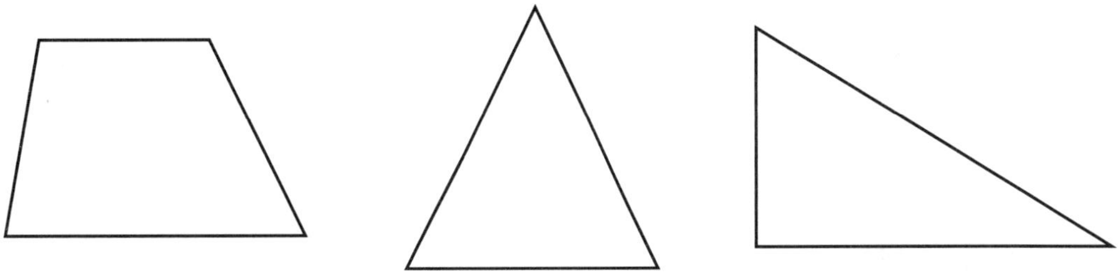

rectangle

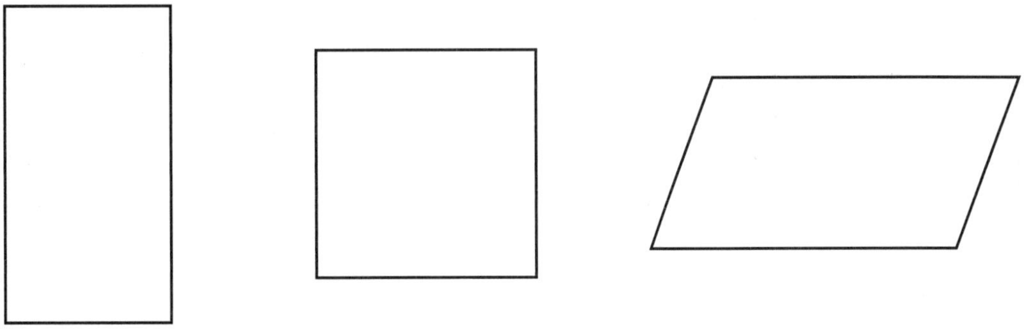

Plane Shapes

Shape Up

A **vertex** is where two lines meet. A **side** is the line between two vertices.

Example:

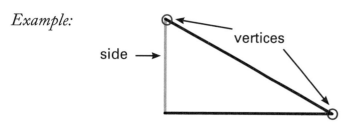

side → vertices

WRITE the number of vertices and sides for each shape.

	Number of Vertices	Number of Sides

Around We Go

Perimeter is the distance around a two-dimensional shape. To find the perimeter, add all of the side lengths. For shapes with sides that are all the same length, multiply the length of one side by the number of sides.

Example:

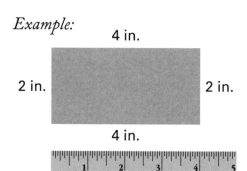

4 + 2 + 4 + 2 = 12
The perimeter of this rectangle is 12 in.

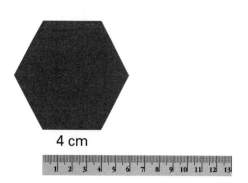

4 x 6 = 24
The perimeter of this hexagon is 24 cm.

WRITE the perimeter of each shape.

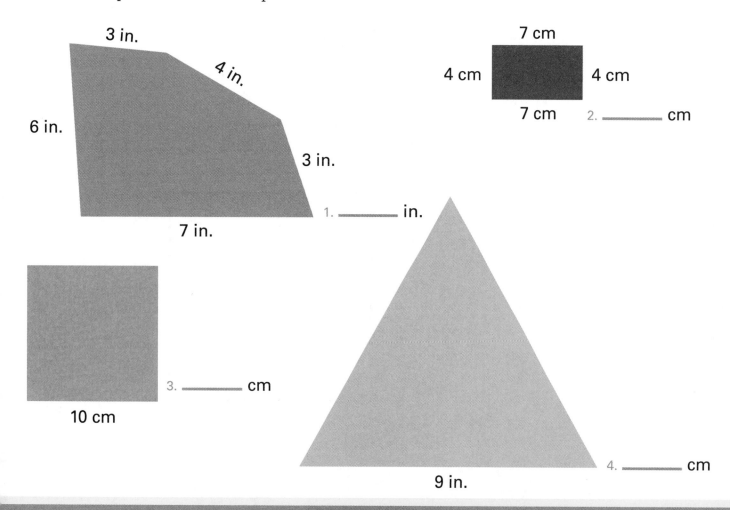

1. _____ in.

2. _____ cm

3. _____ cm

4. _____ cm

Squared Away

Area is the size of the surface of a shape, and it is measured in square units. WRITE the area of each shape.

Example:

1 square unit

To find the area, multiply the height by the width. This rectangle is 2 square units high by 4 square units wide. 2 x 4 = 8.

The area of this rectangle is 8 square units.

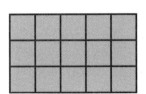

1. _____ square units

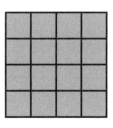

2. _____ square units

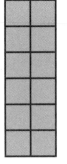

3. _____ square units

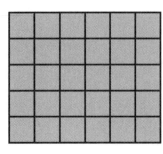

4. _____ square units

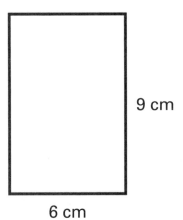

9 cm

6 cm

5. _____ sq cm

5 in.

6. _____ sq in.

Find the Same

CIRCLE the object in each row that is the same shape as the first shape.

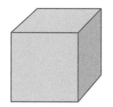   

Odd One Out

CROSS OUT the shape in each row that is **not** the same as the others.

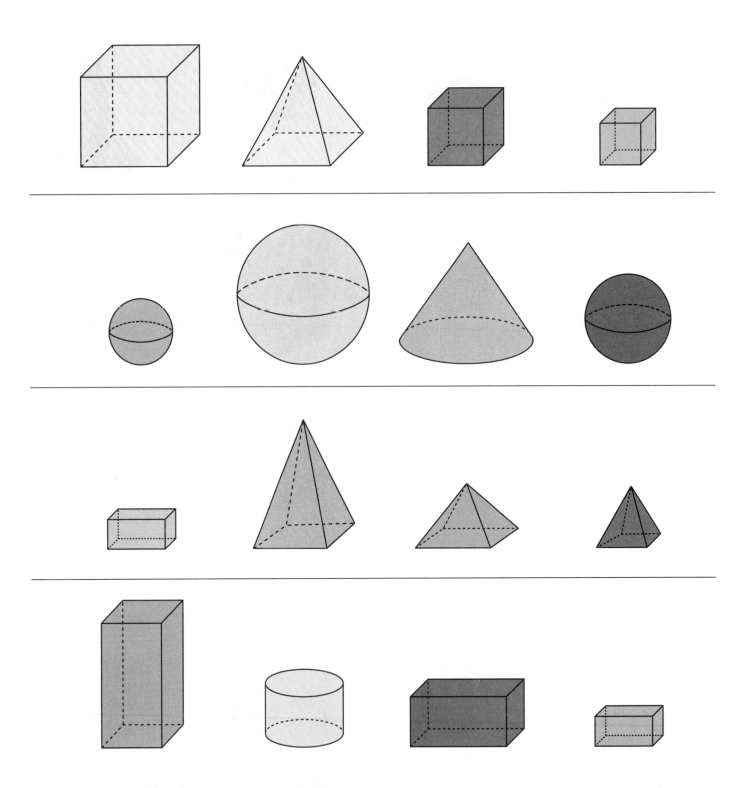

Shape Up

In a three-dimensional shape, a **vertex** is where three or more edges meet. An **edge** is where two sides meet. A **face** is the shape formed by the edges.

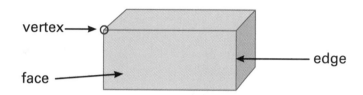

WRITE the number of vertices, edges, and faces for each shape.

	Number of Vertices	Number of Edges	Number of Faces

About Face

CIRCLE all of the shapes that are faces on the three-dimensional shape.

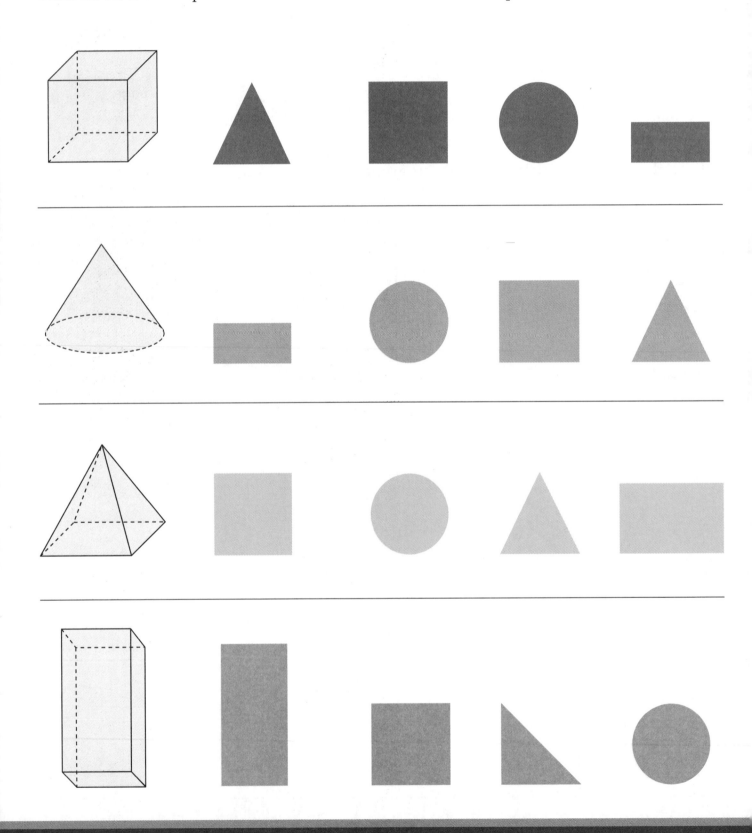

Mirror, Mirror

DRAW a line of symmetry through each picture.

HINT: Some shapes have more than one line of symmetry.

Color Flip

COLOR the pictures so they are symmetrical.

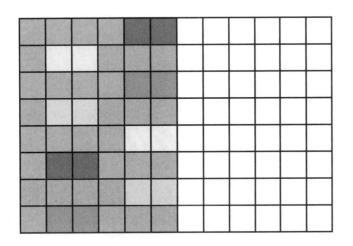

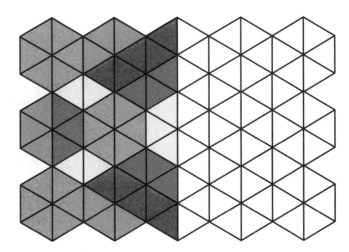

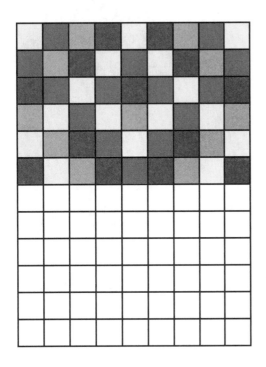

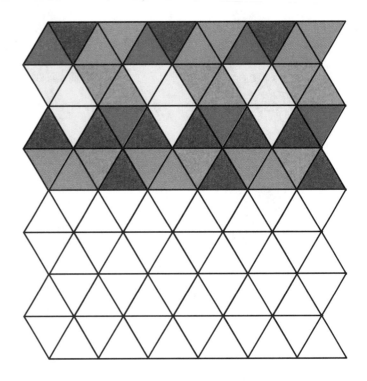

Any Which Way

A **flip**, **slide**, or **turn** has been applied to each shape. WRITE *flip*, *slide*, or *turn* for each pair of shapes.

Example:

flip   slide   turn

1.

2.

3.

4.

5.

6.

7.

8.

Perfect Patterns

A **tessellation** is a repeating pattern of shapes that has no gaps or overlapping shapes. DRAW and COLOR the rest of each tessellation.

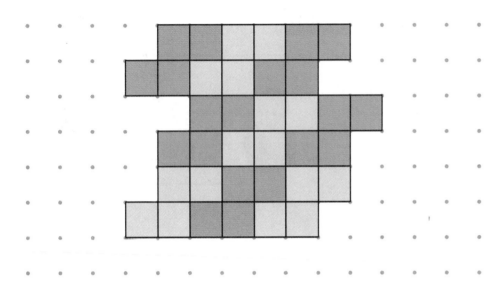

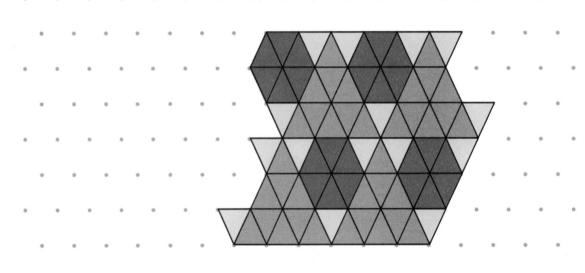

It's about Time

WRITE the time on each clock.

Example:

5 : 37

1. ___ : ___

2. ___ : ___

3. ___ : ___

4. ___ : ___

5. ___ : ___

6. ___ : ___

Watch It!

DRAW a line to connect each watch to a clock that shows the same time.

Set Your Clock

Each clock has the wrong time. DRAW hands to show the correct time on each clock.

HINT: Add time to a clock that is slow, and subtract time from a clock that is fast.

1.

   1 hour and 41 minutes slow   ⟶

2.

   2 hours and 27 minutes slow   ⟶

3.

   1 hour and 16 minutes fast   ⟶

4.

   3 hours and 45 minutes fast   ⟶

Time Difference

WRITE the difference in time between each pair of clocks.

1.

1:17   5:58

_____ hours _____ minutes

2.

10:43   12:47

_____ hours _____ minutes

3.

6:36   9:09

_____ hours _____ minutes

4.

7:24   11:11

_____ hours _____ minutes

Tick Tock, Tick Tock

Jake follows the same schedule every day. How much time does he spend doing each activity in five days?

HINT: Multiply each time by 5.

ONE DAY

Eating	1 hour
Watching TV	1 hour 30 minutes
Going to school	6 hours 45 minutes
Reading	45 minutes
Playing soccer	2 hours 15 minutes
Sleeping	8 hours 20 minutes

FIVE DAYS

1. Eating _____ hours _____ minutes

2. Watching TV _____ hours _____ minutes

3. Going to school _____ hours _____ minutes

4. Reading _____ hours _____ minutes

5. Playing soccer _____ hours _____ minutes

6. Sleeping _____ hours _____ minutes

Mad Dash

WRITE how long it took for each person to run one mile. CIRCLE the person who had the fastest time per mile.

HINT: Divide the total time by the number of miles.

5 miles: 45 minutes

1. 1 mile: _____ minutes

2 miles: 20 minutes

2. 1 mile: _____ minutes

8 miles: 64 minutes

3. 1 mile: _____ minutes

3 miles: 18 minutes

4. 1 mile: _____ minutes

10 miles: 1 hour 10 minutes

5. 1 mile: _____ minutes

7 miles: 56 minutes

6. 1 mile: _____ minutes

Cash Crunch

WRITE the total cost to buy all four items.

HINT: Use the money to help you add.

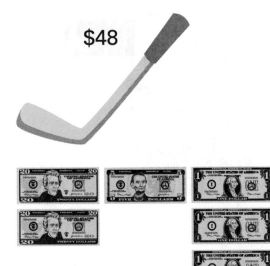

$48

$63.50

$75

$12.25

Total cost _____

Making Change

Using the money to buy each item, how much change will you get back? WRITE the answer for each item.

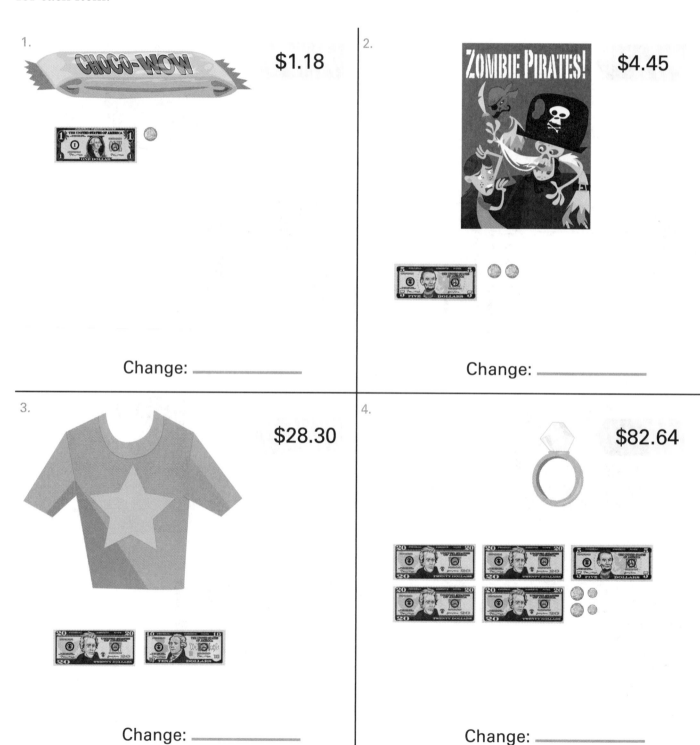

1.

CHOCO-WOW $1.18

Change: _____

2.

ZOMBIE PIRATES! $4.45

Change: _____

3.

$28.30

Change: _____

4.

$82.64

Change: _____

Filling Orders

WRITE the total cost of each order.

Galaxy Burger $5.00

Pluto Burger $7.00

Black Hole Burger $9.00

Out-N-Up BURGERS

Mars Water $1.00

Milky Way Milkshake $3.00

Freaky Fries $2.00

Sunburst Salad $10.00

GUEST CHECK				
Date	Table	Guests	Server	000903
4	Galaxy Burgers			
2	Sunburst Salads			
1	Freaky Fries			
3	Milky Way Milkshakes			
			Total	

GUEST CHECK				
Date	Table	Guests	Server	000904
3	Pluto Burgers			
5	Black Hole Burgers			
2	Milky Way Milkshakes			
4	Mars Waters			
			Total	

GUEST CHECK				
Date	Table	Guests	Server	000905
4	Galaxy Burgers			
9	Pluto Burgers			
3	Sunburst Salads			
6	Freaky Fries			
5	Mars Waters			
			Total	

GUEST CHECK				
Date	Table	Guests	Server	000906
2	Pluto Burgers			
8	Black Hole Burgers			
2	Sunburst Salads			
5	Freaky Fries			
4	Milky Way Milkshakes			
			Total	

Best Price

WRITE the cost of one marble. CIRCLE the bag that has the lowest price for one marble.

1.  $36.00

1 marble: _____

2. $4.50

1 marble: _____

3.  $9.00

1 marble: _____

4.  $20.00

1 marble: _____

5.  $20.00

1 marble: _____

6.  $14.00

1 marble: _____

7. 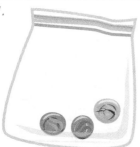 $12.75

1 marble: _____

8.  $24.00

1 marble: _____

Answers

Page 3
1. 5, 0, 8, 1   2. 6, 3, 3, 7
3. 0, 4, 2, 8   4. 9, 9, 6, 3
5. 2, 0, 0, 6   6. 3, 7, 1, 2

Page 4
1. six thousand, four hundred five
2. one thousand, five hundred thirty-eight
3. two thousand, seven hundred eighty
4. four thousand, nine hundred ninety-nine
5. seven thousand, two hundred sixty-three
6. nine thousand, three hundred fourteen
7. 3,576   8. 8,633   9. 5,210
10. 9,891   11. 7,345   12. 1,452

Page 5
1. 3,345   2. 8,229   3. 5,674
4. 1,963   5. 4,516   6. 6,437

Page 6
1. 7,481   2. 2,356   3. 6,292
4. 4,623   5. 9,108   6. 5,534

Page 7
1. <   2. >   3. >
4. <   5. <   6. >
7. >   8. <   9. <
10. >   11. <   12. >
13. >   14. <   15. <

Pages 8
1. >   2. <   3. =
4. >   5. =   6. <

Pages 9
1. 6,672   2. 9,158   3. 5,803
4. 4,910   5. 7,398   6. 3,848

Page 10
1. 4,763   2. 7,848   3. 3,399
4. 6,332   5. 2,165   6. 9,528

Page 11
1. 20   2. 90   3. 40
4. 90   5. 50   6. 80
7. 20   8. 40   9. 500
10. 400   11. 100   12. 800
13. 500   14. 800   15. 600
16. 300

Page 12
1. 7,000   2. 1,000   3. 6,000
4. 8,000   5. 3,000   6. 6,000
7. 9,000   8. 3,000   9. 2,000
10. 4,000   11. 8,000   12. 6,000
13. 4,000   14. 3,000   15. 7,000
16. 4,000

Page 13
Check:
1. $16   2. $240   3. $3,200

Page 14
Check: 167

Page 15
1. 83   2. 58   3. 99
4. 67   5. 87   6. 49
7. 93   8. 66   9. 59
10. 48   11. 76   12. 97

Page 16
1. 55   2. 41   3. 10
4. 21   5. 47   6. 15
7. 32   8. 53   9. 31
10. 26   11. 68   12. 12

Page 17
1. 589   2. 894   3. 558
4. 467   5. 977   6. 742

Page 18
1. 447   2. 179   3. 356
4. 895   5. 699   6. 552
7. 748   8. 969   9. 773
10. 496   11. 949   12. 297
13. 664   14. 585   15. 794
16. 476

Page 19
1.
$$
\begin{array}{r}
516 \\
+ 349 \\
\end{array}
$$
500 + 300 = 800
10 + 40 = 50
6 + 9 = + 15
865

2.
$$
\begin{array}{r}
399 \\
+ 174 \\
\end{array}
$$
300 + 100 = 400
90 + 70 = 160
9 + 4 = + 13
573

3.
$$
\begin{array}{r}
472 \\
+ 225 \\
\end{array}
$$
400 + 200 = 600
70 + 20 = 90
2 + 5 = + 7
697

4.
$$
\begin{array}{r}
534 \\
+ 177 \\
\end{array}
$$
500 + 100 = 600
30 + 70 = 100
4 + 7 = + 11
711

5.
$$
\begin{array}{r}
290 \\
+ 636 \\
\end{array}
$$
200 + 600 = 800
90 + 30 = 120
0 + 6 = + 6
926

6.
$$
\begin{array}{r}
198 \\
+ 184 \\
\end{array}
$$
100 + 100 = 200
90 + 80 = 170
8 + 4 = + 12
382

7.
$$
\begin{array}{r}
427 \\
+ 296 \\
\end{array}
$$
400 + 200 = 600
20 + 90 = 110
7 + 6 = + 13
723

8.
$$
\begin{array}{r}
688 \\
+ 263 \\
\end{array}
$$
600 + 200 = 800
80 + 60 = 140
8 + 3 = + 11
951

Page 20
1. 911   2. 645   3. 791
4. 783   5. 421   6. 505
7. 832   8. 512   9. 932
10. 820   11. 700   12. 657

Page 21
1. 152   2. 423   3. 305
4. 121   5. 211   6. 446

Page 22
1. 714   2. 352   3. 824
4. 513   5. 261   6. 562
7. 442   8. 104   9. 137
10. 318   11. 331   12. 521
13. 705   14. 374   15. 429
16. 680

Page 23
1. 184   2. 208   3. 364
4. 148   5. 59   6. 289

Page 24
1. 288   2. 452   3. 696
4. 117   5. 228   6. 176
7. 245   8. 87   9. 689
10. 55   11. 148   12. 325

Page 25
1. 283   2. 175   3. 443
4. 246   5. 185   6. 19
7. 569   8. 657   9. 335
10. 149   11. 298   12. 72

Page 26
1. 350   2. 468   3. 279
4. 176   5. 356   6. 123
7. 286   8. 98   9. 293
10. 437   11. 89   12. 269
13. 122   14. 687   15. 162
16. 361

Page 27
1. 20   2. 17   3. 25
4. 50   5. 69   6. 185
7. 136   8. 143   9. 249
10. 513   11. 721   12. 800
13. 170   14. 226   15. 718
16. 959

Page 28
1. 161   2. 519   3. 790
4. 964   5. 152   6. 773
7. 625   8. 870

Page 29
1. 5,286   2. 3,737   3. 9,383
4. 7,820   5. 6,659   6. 4,745
7. 1,815   8. 4,006   9. 2,897
10. 7,589   11. 5,553   12. 6,738
13. 6,221   14. 3,426   15. 4,113
16. 9,805

Page 30
1. 6,511   2. 1,326   3. 4,484
4. 5,073   5. 9,262   6. 7,314
7. 4,939   8. 1,992   9. 1,121
10. 5,470   11. 3,442   12. 4,117
13. 3,478   14. 2,779   15. 7,454
16. 2,909

Page 31
1.
$$
\begin{array}{r}
423 \\
+ 271 \\
\hline
694
\end{array}
\qquad
\begin{array}{r}
400 \\
+ 200 \\
\hline
600
\end{array}
$$

2.
$$
\begin{array}{r}
190 \\
+ 724 \\
\hline
914
\end{array}
\qquad
\begin{array}{r}
100 \\
+ 700 \\
\hline
800
\end{array}
$$

3.
$$
\begin{array}{r}
2,385 \\
+ 612 \\
\hline
2,997
\end{array}
\qquad
\begin{array}{r}
2,000 \\
+ 600 \\
\hline
2,600
\end{array}
$$

4.
$$
\begin{array}{r}
8,732 \\
+ 958 \\
\hline
9,690
\end{array}
\qquad
\begin{array}{r}
8,000 \\
+ 900 \\
\hline
8,900
\end{array}
$$

5.
$$
\begin{array}{r}
3,361 \\
+4,518 \\
\hline
7,879
\end{array}
\qquad
\begin{array}{r}
3,000 \\
+ 4,000 \\
\hline
7,000
\end{array}
$$

6.
$$
\begin{array}{r}
2,112 \\
+1,308 \\
\hline
3,420
\end{array}
\qquad
\begin{array}{r}
2,000 \\
+1,000 \\
\hline
3,000
\end{array}
$$

Page 32
1.
$$
\begin{array}{r}
872 \\
- 661 \\
\hline
211
\end{array}
\qquad
\begin{array}{r}
800 \\
-600 \\
\hline
200
\end{array}
$$

2.
$$
\begin{array}{r}
925 \\
- 629 \\
\hline
296
\end{array}
\qquad
\begin{array}{r}
900 \\
-600 \\
\hline
300
\end{array}
$$

3.
$$
\begin{array}{r}
6,734 \\
- 322 \\
\hline
6,412
\end{array}
\qquad
\begin{array}{r}
6,000 \\
- 300 \\
\hline
5,700
\end{array}
$$

4.
$$
\begin{array}{r}
1,283 \\
- 564 \\
\hline
719
\end{array}
\qquad
\begin{array}{r}
1,000 \\
- 500 \\
\hline
500
\end{array}
$$

5.
$$
\begin{array}{r}
4,826 \\
-1,711 \\
\hline
3,115
\end{array}
\qquad
\begin{array}{r}
4,000 \\
-1,000 \\
\hline
3,000
\end{array}
$$

6.
$$
\begin{array}{r}
9,382 \\
-7,449 \\
\hline
1,933
\end{array}
\qquad
\begin{array}{r}
9,000 \\
-7,000 \\
\hline
2,000
\end{array}
$$

Page 33
1.
$$
\begin{array}{r}
436 \\
+ 251 \\
\hline
687
\end{array}
\qquad
\begin{array}{r}
400 \\
+ 300 \\
\hline
700
\end{array}
$$

2.
$$
\begin{array}{r}
166 \\
+ 108 \\
\hline
274
\end{array}
\qquad
\begin{array}{r}
200 \\
+ 100 \\
\hline
300
\end{array}
$$

3.
$$
\begin{array}{r}
3,524 \\
+ 367 \\
\hline
3,891
\end{array}
\qquad
\begin{array}{r}
3,500 \\
+ 400 \\
\hline
3,900
\end{array}
$$

4.
$$
\begin{array}{r}
7,539 \\
+ 616 \\
\hline
8,155
\end{array}
\qquad
\begin{array}{r}
7,500 \\
+ 600 \\
\hline
8,100
\end{array}
$$

5.
$$
\begin{array}{r}
2,345 \\
+ 2,354 \\
\hline
4,699
\end{array}
\qquad
\begin{array}{r}
2,300 \\
+ 2,400 \\
\hline
4,700
\end{array}
$$

6.
$$
\begin{array}{r}
4,181 \\
+1,423 \\
\hline
5,604
\end{array}
\qquad
\begin{array}{r}
4,200 \\
+ 1,400 \\
\hline
5,600
\end{array}
$$

Answers

Page 34
1.
878 900
−223 −200
655 700

2.
795 800
−519 −500
276 300

3.
6,428 6,400
− 411 − 400
6,017 6,000

4.
4,493 4,500
− 897 − 900
3,596 3,600

5.
8,781 8,800
−6,447 −6,400
2,334 2,400

6.
7,064 7,100
−1,815 −1,800
5,249 5,300

Page 35
1. 4 2. 12
3. 24 4. 16

Page 36
1. 10 2. 8
3. 5 4. 4

Page 37
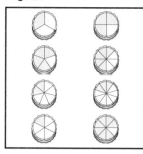

Page 38
1. 8 2. 12 3. 4
4. 14 5. 6

Page 39
1. 15 2. 27 3. 21
4. 24 5. 40

Page 40
1. 20 2. 5 3. 35
4. 30 5. 10 6. 45
7. 25 8. 40 9. 50
10. 15

Page 41
1. 6 2. 0 3. 3
4. 0 5. 10 6. 0
7. 5 8. 0 9. 1
10. 0 11. 9 12. 0
13. 7 14. 0 15. 8
16. 0 17. 2 18. 0

Page 42
1. 28 2. 30 3. 48
4. 36 5. 60

Page 43
1. 10 2. 32 3. 100
4. 27 5. 35 6. 6
7. 30 8. 0 9. 12
10. 49 11. 54 12. 25
13. 16 14. 36 15. 21
16. 0 17. 64 18. 2

Page 44
1. 4 2. 35 3. 24
4. 12 5. 45 6. 20
7. 36 8. 0 9. 8
10. 81 11. 28 12. 15
13. 80 14. 0 15. 36
16. 30 17. 16 18. 16
19. 21 20. 72 21. 8
22. 1 23. 18 24. 45
25. 20 26. 40 27. 0
28. 18 29. 50 30. 9

Page 45
1. 6 2. 10 3. 4

Page 46
1. 6 2. 4
3. 2 4. 8

Page 47
1. 3 2. 5
3. 9 4. 6

Page 48
1. 6 2. 4 3. 5
4. 9 5. 2

Page 49
1. 8 2. 3 3. 10
4. 7 5. 7 6. 2
7. 7 8. 8 9. 8
10. 6 11. 9 12. 6
13. 9 14. 3 15. 7
16. 3 17. 4 18. 10

Page 50
1. 4 2. 10 3. 2
4. 9 5. 8 6. 5
7. 9 8. 7 9. 6
10. 9 11. 4 12. 3
13. 3 14. 5 15. 4
16. 6 17. 8 18. 8
19. 3 20. 10 21. 9
22. 7 23. 9 24. 7
25. 9 26. 2 27. 10
28. 5 29. 8 30. 4

Page 51
1. 1, 2, 4
2. 1, 2, 3, 6
3. 1, 3, 9
4. 1, 2, 3, 4, 6, 12
5. 1, 3, 5, 15
6. 1, 2, 4, 8, 16
7. 1, 2, 3, 6, 9, 18

Page 52
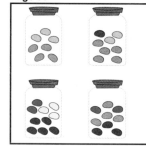

Page 53
1. $\frac{1}{2}$ 2. $\frac{3}{4}$ 3. $\frac{2}{3}$
4. $\frac{2}{5}$ 5. $\frac{3}{8}$ 6. $\frac{5}{6}$

Page 54
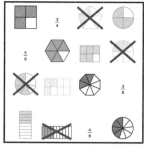

Page 55
1. $\frac{2}{3}$ 2. $\frac{5}{6}$ 3. $\frac{1}{4}$
4. $\frac{4}{7}$ 5. $\frac{6}{8}$ 6. $\frac{1}{10}$
7. $\frac{6}{9}$ 8. $\frac{3}{5}$

Page 56
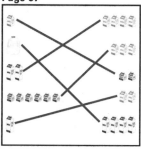

Page 57
1. $\frac{4}{8}$ 2. $\frac{1}{5}$ 3. $\frac{7}{9}$
4. $\frac{2}{6}$ 5. $\frac{6}{10}$ 6. $\frac{3}{7}$

Page 58

Page 59
1. $\frac{3}{7}$ 2. $\frac{5}{7}$ 3. $\frac{2}{3}$
4. $\frac{2}{4}$ 5. $\frac{1}{3}$ 6. $\frac{3}{4}$

Page 60

Page 61
$\frac{1}{6}$ $\frac{1}{5}$
$\frac{4}{7}$ $\frac{3}{8}$
$\frac{1}{4}$ $\frac{2}{9}$
$\frac{7}{10}$ $\frac{7}{8}$

Page 62
1. > 2. > 3. <
4. = 5. < 6. >
7. < 8. < 9. >
10. > 11. > 12. =

Page 63
1. 2, 5 2. 5, 13
3. 3, 8 4. 4, 10

Page 64
1. 3, 8 2. 1, 3 3. 5, 13
4. 2, 5 5. 4, 11 6. 6, 15

Page 65
1. inch 2. inch 3. foot
4. foot 5. yard

Page 66
1. centimeter
2. meter
3. centimeter
4. meter
5. meter
6. centimeter

Page 67

Page 68
1. gallon 2. cup
3. pint 4. gallon
5. cup 6. quart
7. gallon 8. pint

Page 69

Page 70
1. milliliter   2. liter
3. milliliter   4. milliliter
5. liter   6. milliliter
7. liter   8. liter

Page 71

Page 72
1. ounce   2. pound
3. ounce   4. pound
5. pound   6. ounce
7. ounce   8. pound

Page 73

Page 74
1. gram   2. kilogram
3. gram   4. gram
5. kilogram   6. gram
7. gram   8. kilogram

Page 75
1. 68, 20   2. 41, 5
3. 50, 10   4. 95, 35
5. 32, 0   6. 77, 25

Page 76

Page 77

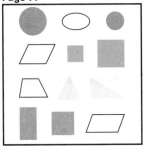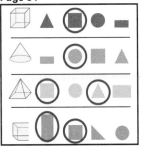

Page 78

	Number of vertices	Number of sides
	3	3
	4	4
	3	3
	6	6
	4	4

Page 79
1. 23   2. 22
3. 40   4. 27

Page 80
1. 15   2. 16
3. 12   4. 30
5. 54   6. 25

Page 81

Page 82

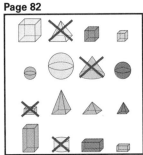

Page 83

	Number of vertices	Number of edges	Number of faces
	8	12	6
	5	8	5
	8	12	6
	4	6	4

Page 84

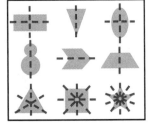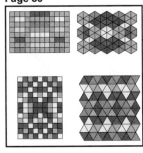

Page 85

Page 86

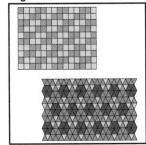

Page 87
1. fllp   2. turn
3. slide   4. flip
5. turn   6. slide
7. flip   8. turn

Page 88

Page 89
1. 10:02   2. 6:18
3. 2:44   4. 9:51
5. 11:27   6. 3:33

Page 90

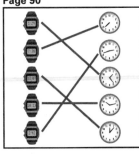

Page 91

Page 92
1. 4, 41   2. 2, 4
3. 2, 33   4. 3, 47

Page 93
1. 5, 0   2. 7, 30
3. 33, 45   4. 3, 45
5. 11, 15   6. 41, 40

Page 94
1. 9   2. 10   3. 8
4. 6   5. 7   6. 8

Fastest time per mile:

Page 95
$ 198.75

Page 96
1. $ 0.07   2. $ 1.05
3. $ 1.70   4. $ 3.06

Page 97

	GUEST CHECK	
		000903
4	Galaxy Burgers	$20.00
2	Sunburst Salads	$20.00
1	Freaky Fries	$2.00
3	Milky Way Milkshakes	$9.00
	Total	$51.00

	GUEST CHECK	
		000904
3	Pluto Burgers	$21.00
5	Black Hole Burgers	$45.00
2	Milky Way Milkshakes	$6.00
4	Mars Waters	$4.00
	Total	$76.00

Answers

Page 97 (continued)

	GUEST CHECK		
			000905
4	Galaxy Burgers		$20.00
9	Pluto Burgers		$63.00
3	Sunburst Salads		$30.00
6	Freaky Fries		$12.00
5	Mars Waters		$5.00
		Total	$130.00

	GUEST CHECK		
			000906
2	Pluto Burgers		$14.00
8	Black Hole Burgers		$72.00
2	Sunburst Salads		$20.00
5	Freaky Fries		$10.00
4	Milky Way Milkshakes		$12.00
		Total	$128.00

Page 98

1. $6.00   2. $2.25
3. $1.00   4. $5.00
5. $2.00   6. $2.00
7. $4.25   8. $3.00

Lowest price for
1 marble:

3rd Grade
Math
Games & Puzzles

Safe Crackers

WRITE the amount of money you see in each picture. Then WRITE the digit in the thousands place of each number from smallest to largest to find the combination for the safe.

$ 1,283
1

$ _____
2

$ _____
3

$ _____
4

$ _____
5

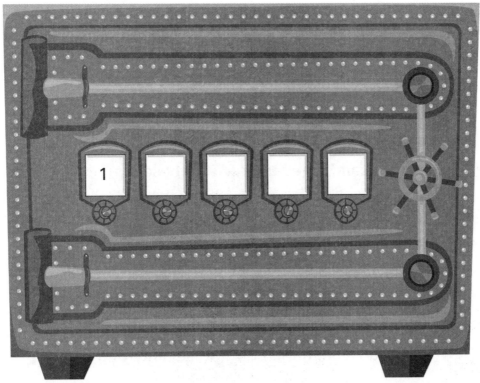

1

Place Value

Criss Cross

READ the clues, and WRITE the numbers in the puzzle.

ACROSS

1. three thousand, two hundred nineteen
4. six thousand fifty-two
6. eight thousand, five hundred seven
9. one thousand, three hundred eighty-eight
10. seven thousand, four hundred forty-six
11. nine thousand, eight hundred fifty-three
13. four thousand, nine hundred ninety
15. two thousand, one hundred sixty-nine
18. three thousand, four hundred seventeen
19. five thousand, two hundred sixty-two

DOWN

2. two thousand, four hundred forty-eight
3. nine thousand, six hundred thirty
5. two thousand, seven hundred forty-three
7. five thousand, six hundred fifty-four
8. four thousand, eight hundred twenty-three
9. one thousand, one hundred ninety-seven
10. seven thousand eighty-four
12. five thousand, two hundred sixteen
14. nine thousand, one hundred twenty-four
16. six thousand, seven hundred fifty-five
17. four thousand, five hundred sixty-eight
18. three thousand, three hundred seventy-one

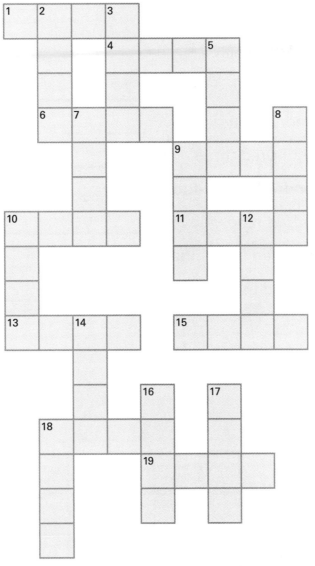

Number Search

WRITE each number. Then CIRCLE it in the puzzle.

HINT: Numbers are across and down only.

1. seven thousand, six hundred twenty-six   <u>7,626</u>

2. four thousand, one hundred fifty-five

3. eight thousand, three hundred three

4. one thousand, nine hundred eighty-four

5. six thousand, four hundred ninety-seven

6. two thousand, eight hundred forty-nine

7. five thousand, two hundred twenty-four

2	4	1	5	5	5
7	3	9	8	2	5
2	9	8	6	2	1
8	6	4	9	7	9
4	0	1	8	6	2
9	9	5	2	2	4
0	6	7	5	6	3
8	3	0	3	0	1

Totally Tangled

Each numbered circle is connected to another numbered circle. FIND the pairs of numbers, and COLOR the circle with the smaller number.

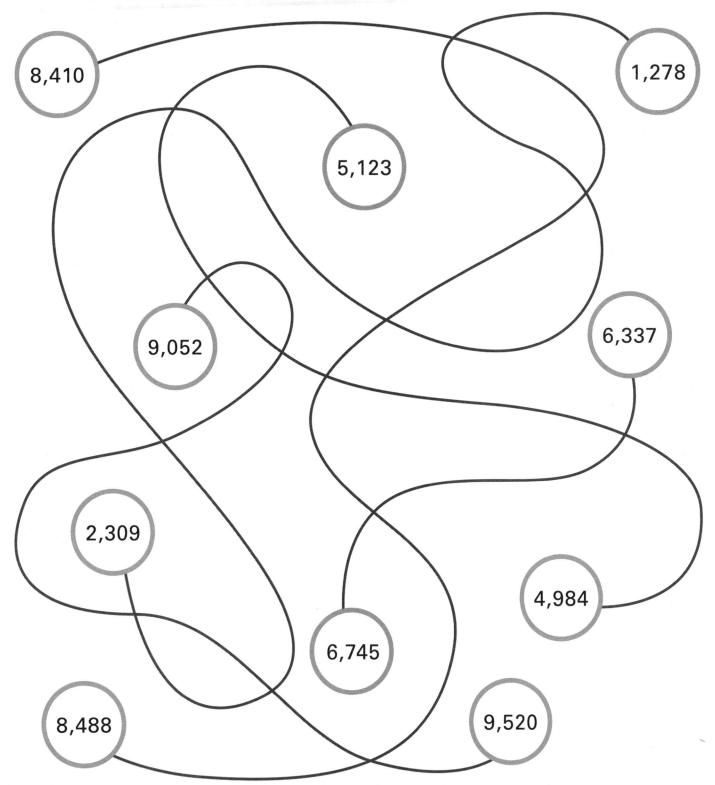

Win Big

Wherever two boxes point to one box, WRITE the larger number. START at the sides and work toward the center to see which number will win big.

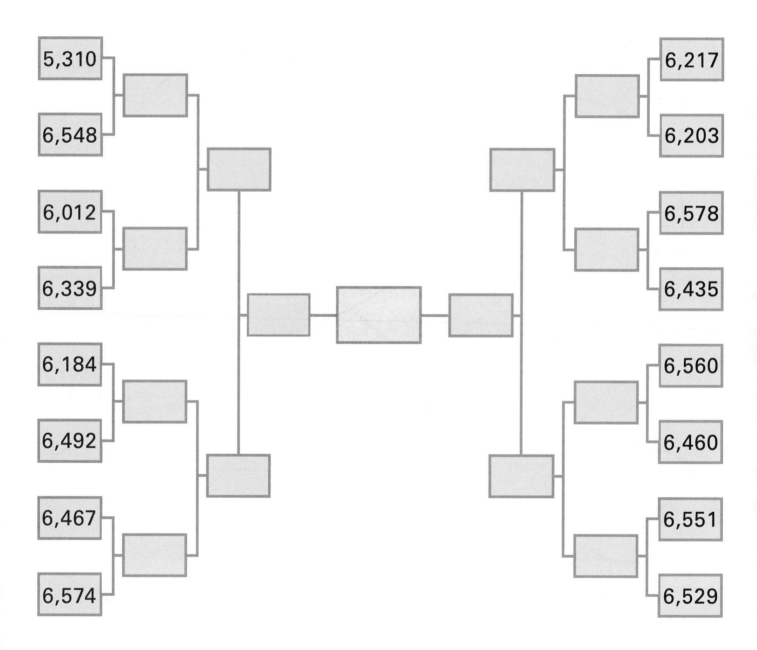

Totally Tangled

Each numbered circle is connected to another numbered circle. FIND the pairs of numbers, and COLOR the circle with the larger number.

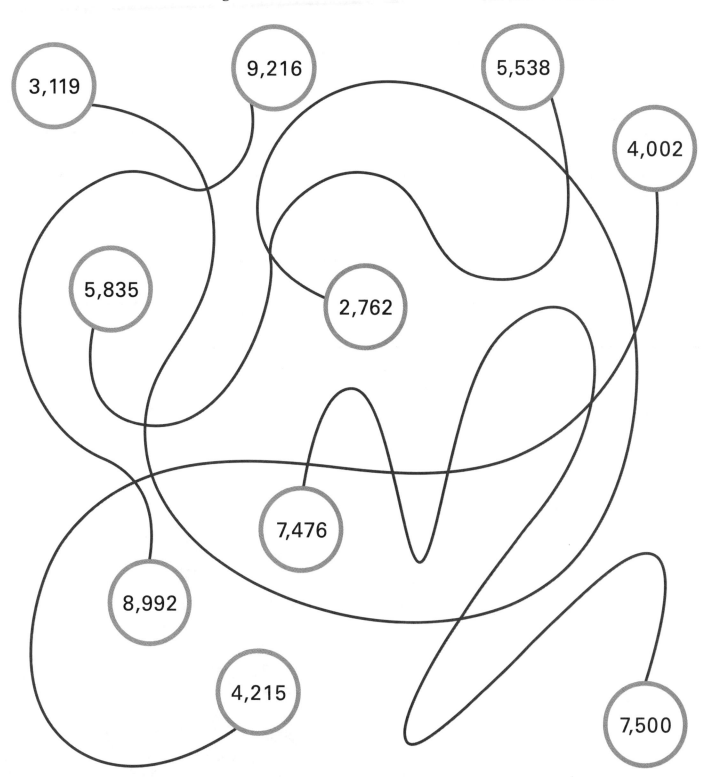

The Scrambler

WRITE all of the different numbers that can be made from the four digits. Order them from smallest to largest.

1   3   6   8

1,368 _____   1,386 _____   _____   _____

_____   _____   _____   _____

_____   _____   _____   _____

_____   _____   _____   _____

_____   _____   _____   _____

_____   _____   _____   _____

Totally Tangled

Each numbered circle is connected to another numbered circle. FIND the pairs of numbers, and COLOR any pair that connects a number with that number correctly rounded to the nearest hundred.

HINT: Numbers that end in 1 through 49 get rounded down to the nearest hundred. Numbers that end in 50 through 99 get rounded up to the nearest hundred.

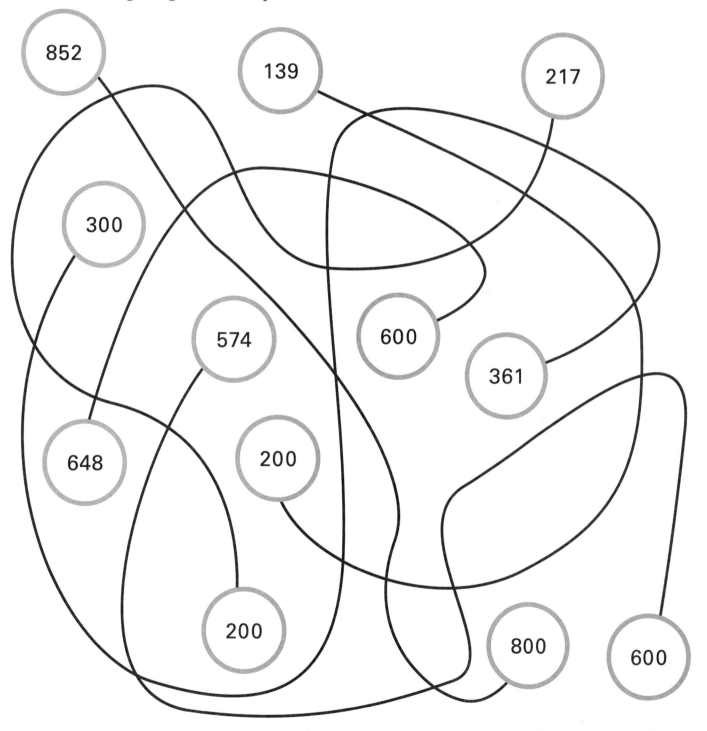

Just Right

WRITE each number to correctly complete the sentences. There may be more than one place to put a number, but you need to use every number.

HINT: Numbers that end in 1 through 499 get rounded down to the nearest thousand. Numbers that end in 500 through 999 get rounded up to the nearest thousand.

| 5,845 | 5,136 | 4,498 | 5,755 | 4,375 |
| 5,213 | 5,742 | 5,178 | 4,372 | |

1. _____ rounded to the nearest thousand is 6,000.

2. _____ rounded to the nearest hundred is 4,400.

3. _____ rounded to the nearest ten is 5,850.

4. _____ rounded to the nearest thousand is 4,000.

5. _____ rounded to the nearest hundred is 5,200.

6. _____ rounded to the nearest thousand is 5,000.

7. _____ rounded to the nearest hundred is 5,700.

8. _____ rounded to the nearest ten is 4,380.

9. _____ rounded to the nearest ten is 5,210.

Fitting In

ESTIMATE how many jellybeans are needed to fill the circle. WRITE your estimate. Then turn the page to CHECK your estimate.

Estimate: _____

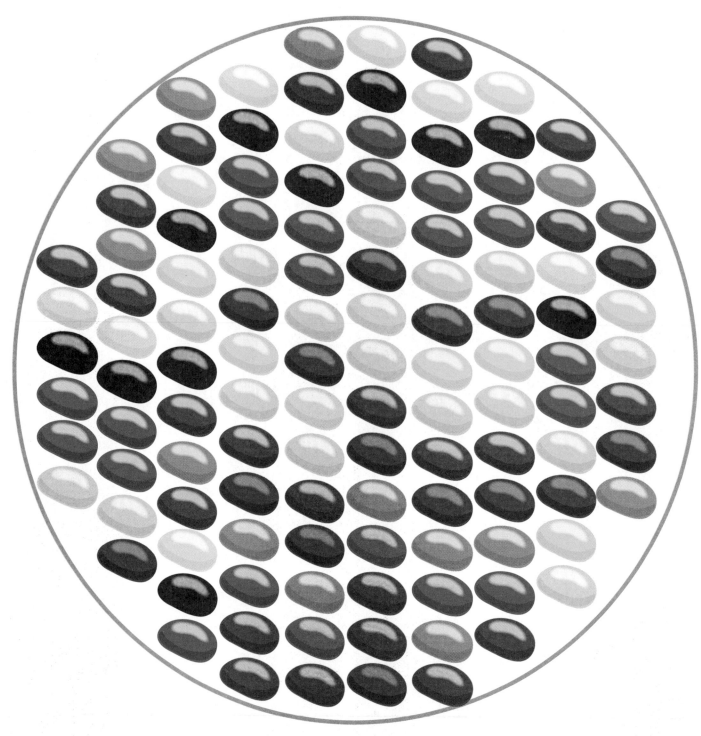

Check: _____

Skipping Stones

DRAW a path by skip counting by 12 to cross the river.

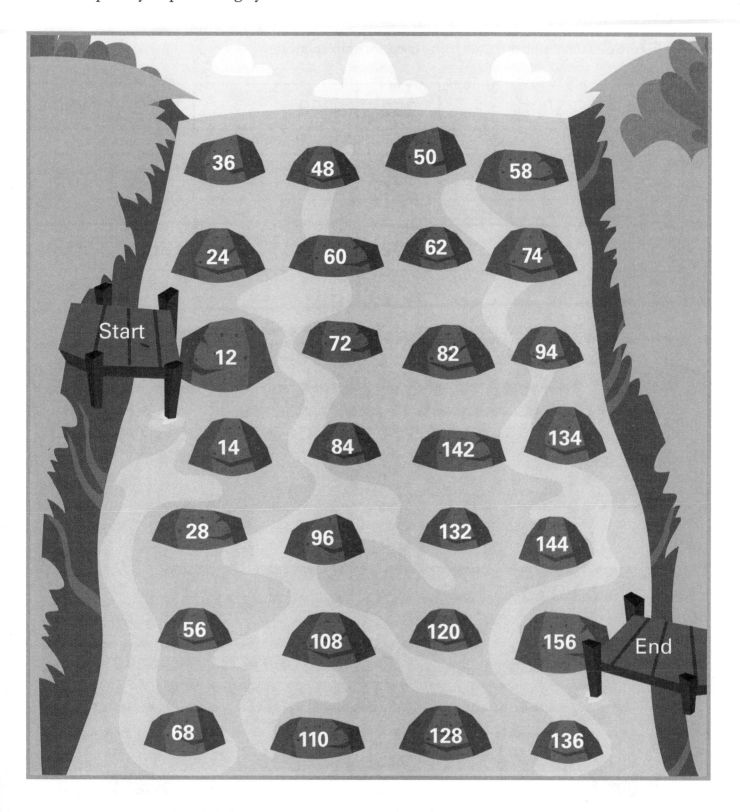

Safe Crackers

WRITE the missing numbers in each pattern. Then WRITE those numbers from smallest to largest to find the right combination for the safe.

HINT: Figure out the number that is being used for skip counting.

1.

231	238		252	259		273	280

2.

	155	170	185	200	215		245

3.

255		273	282	291		309	318

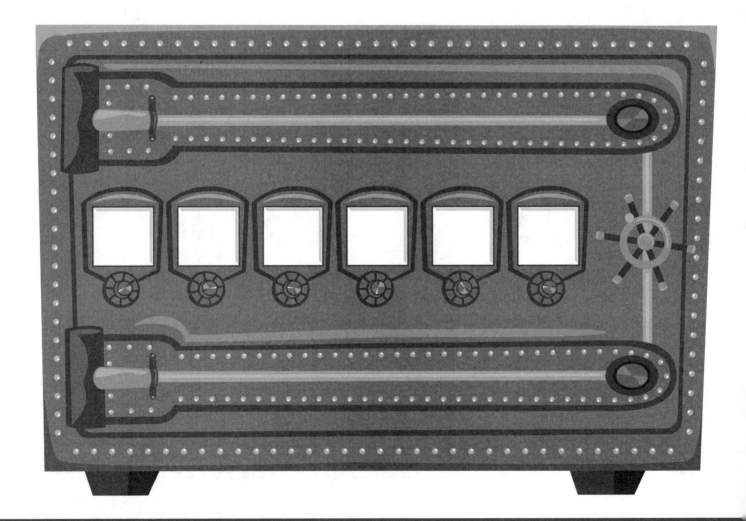

Who Am I?

READ the clues, and CIRCLE the mystery number.

HINT: Cross out any number that does not match the clues.

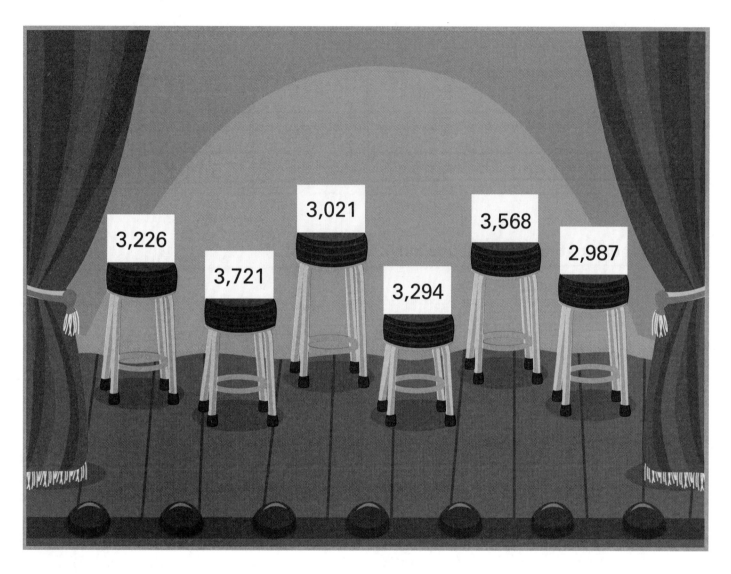

I am more than 3,000.

I am less than 3,700.

When rounded to the nearest thousand, I'm 3,000.

I have a 2 in the hundreds place.

When rounded to the nearest hundred, I'm 3,300.

Who am I?

Last One Standing

CROSS OUT each number that does not match the clues until one number is left.

HINT: Follow the clues in order. The last number left should match all of the clues.

5,511	4,756	5,731	5,648
6,328	5,182	6,495	5,963
5,657	5,674	5,300	5,520
5,609	5,523	5,299	5,682

When rounded to the nearest thousand, it is 6,000.

It has a 5 in the thousands place.

It is the biggest number in its row.

It has a 6 in the hundreds place.

When rounded to the nearest ten, it is 5,670.

Missing Middles

WRITE the number missing from the center square.

1.

	30	
	+	
12 +		= 55
	=	
	73	

2.

	65	
	+	
46 +		= 68
	=	
	87	

3.

	17	
	+	
38 +		= 89
	=	
	68	

4.

	24	
	+	
47 +		= 83
	=	
	60	

5.

	29	
	+	
16 +		= 81
	=	
	94	

6.

	36	
	+	
55 +		= 72
	=	
	53	

Crossing Paths

WRITE the missing numbers.

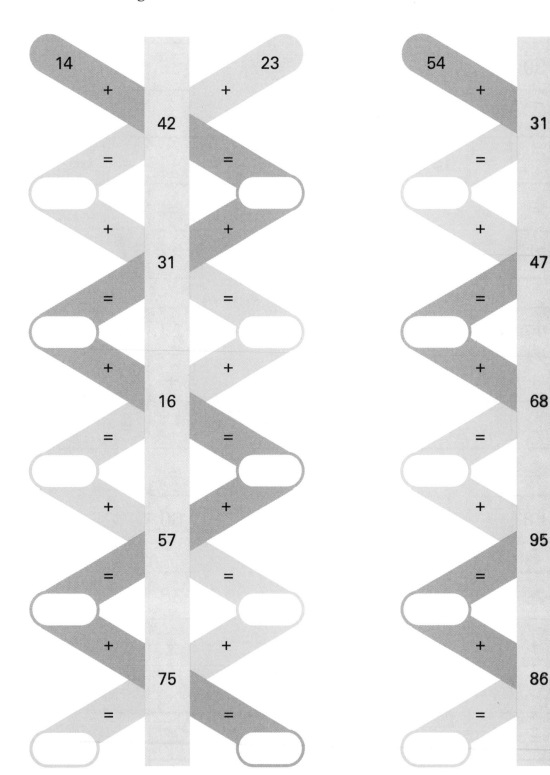

Super Square

WRITE numbers in the empty squares to finish all of the addition problems.

58	+	92	=	
+		+		+
134	+		=	
=		=		=
	+	341	=	

Adding

Pipe Down

WRITE the missing number. Then FOLLOW the pipe, and WRITE the same number in the next problem.

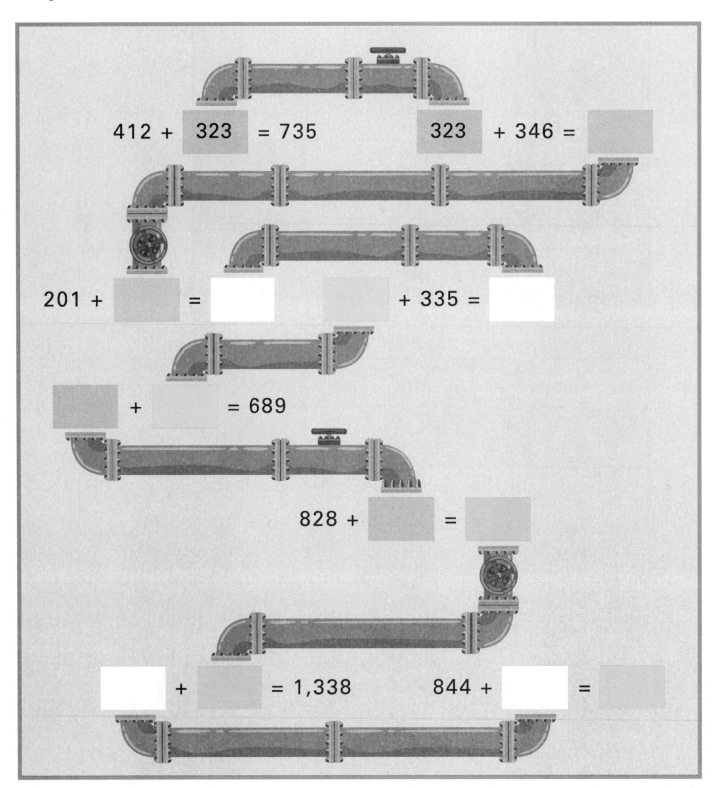

412 + 323 = 735

323 + 346 =

201 + ___ = ___

___ + 335 = ___

___ + ___ = 689

828 + ___ = ___

___ + ___ = 1,338

844 + ___ = ___

Code Breaker

SOLVE each problem. WRITE the letter that matches each sum to solve the riddle.

7,165 + 63	1,233 + 29	5,906 + 44	3,825 + 18	2,775 + 619	8,375 + 261
1	2	3	4	5	6
Y	F	C	I	E	O

4,632 + 860	2,169 + 361	7,335 +1,427	5,079 +4,838	6,874 +2,382	4,631 +1,767
7	8	9	10	11	12
R	D	T	N	A	U

Why does a calculator make a good friend?

It's a ____ ____ ____ ____ ____ ____
      1,262 5,492 3,843 3,394 9,917 2,530

____ ____ ____   ____ ____ ____
7,228 8,636 6,398   5,950 9,256 9,917

____ ____ ____ ____ ____   ____ ____
5,950 8,636 6,398 9,917 8,762   8,636 9,917

Adding

Number Nudge

For each set of problems, WRITE the missing numbers so that the answers are correct.

1,728   3,185   2,037   1,410

1. 1,182 + _____ = 2,910
2. 3,205 + _____ = 5,242
3. 2,732 + _____ + _____ = 7,327

3,218   2,541   2,959   1,588

4. 4,201 + _____ = 7,160
5. 5,570 + _____ = 8,111
6. 3,321 + _____ + _____ = 8,127

1,549   879   1,713   1,236   1,188   950

7. 4,201 + _____ = 5,389
8. 5,570 + _____ = 7,119
9. 3,321 + _____ + _____ = 6,270

Missing Middles

WRITE the number missing from the center square

1.

57

−

33 − ☐ = 21

=

45

2.

94

−

68 − ☐ = 6

=

32

3.

75

−

46 − ☐ = 12

=

41

4.

53

−

92 − ☐ = 43

=

4

5.

81

−

74 − ☐ = 19

=

26

6.

42

−

67 − ☐ = 39

=

14

Crossing Paths

WRITE the missing numbers.

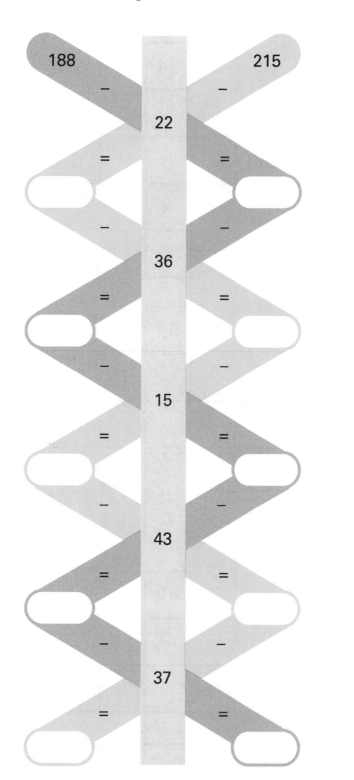

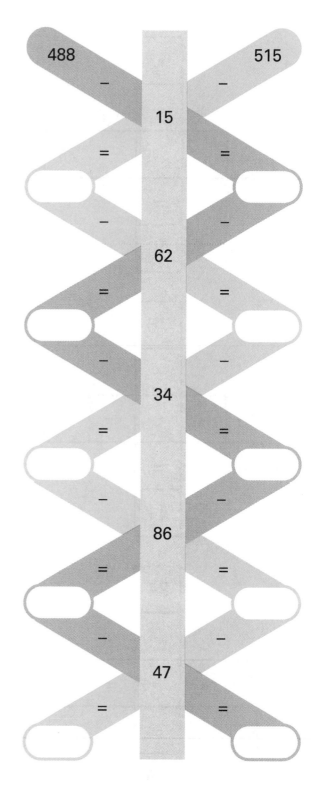

Super Square

WRITE numbers in the empty squares to finish all of the subtraction problems.

492	–		=	313
–		–		–
261	–		=	
=		=		=
	–	132	=	

Pipe Down

WRITE the missing number. Then FOLLOW the pipe, and WRITE the same number in the next problem.

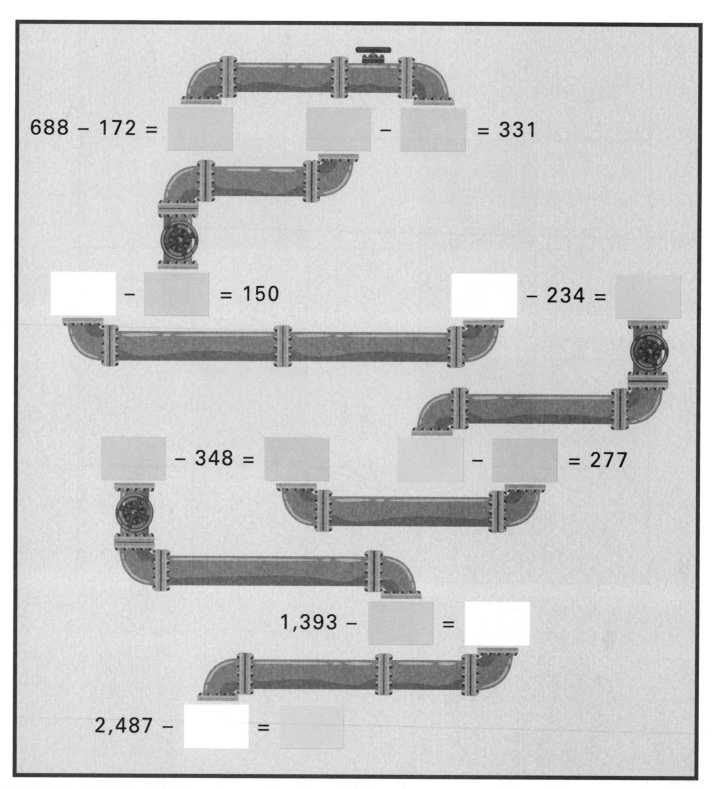

688 – 172 = ☐ ☐ – ☐ = 331

☐ – ☐ = 150 ☐ – 234 = ☐

☐ – 348 = ☐ ☐ – ☐ = 277

1,393 – ☐ = ☐

2,487 – ☐ = ☐

Code Breaker

SOLVE each problem. WRITE the letter that matches each difference to solve the riddle.

3,969 − 72	2,214 − 58	8,028 − 46	5,389 − 95	6,431 − 578	7,983 − 294
1	2	3	4	5	6
T	S	I	H	B	N

3,880 − 403	4,752 − 166	8,121 −2,742	5,592 −1,226	9,412 −3,242	4,008 −2,771
7	8	9	10	11	12
U	R	D	A	C	E

How do you turn a cookie into a cook?

___ ___ ___ ___ ___ ___ ___ ___
2,156 3,477 5,853 3,897 4,586 4,366 6,170 3,897

___ ___ ___   ___   ___ ___ ___   ___ .
3,897 5,294 1,237   7,982   4,366 7,689 5,379   1,237

Number Nudge

For each set of problems, WRITE the missing numbers so that the answers are correct.

3,123	1,014	992	1,258

1. $7,525 - \underline{\hspace{2cm}} = 6,533$
2. $7,398 - \underline{\hspace{2cm}} = 4,275$
3. $6,651 - \underline{\hspace{2cm}} - \underline{\hspace{2cm}} = 4,379$

2,591	2,367	2,004	1,702

4. $5,227 - \underline{\hspace{2cm}} = 2,860$
5. $4,510 - \underline{\hspace{2cm}} = 2,506$
6. $6,807 - \underline{\hspace{2cm}} - \underline{\hspace{2cm}} = 2,514$

3,921	3,289	1,542	4,330

7. $9,776 - \underline{\hspace{2cm}} = 6,487$
8. $8,823 - \underline{\hspace{2cm}} = 4,493$
9. $9,504 - \underline{\hspace{2cm}} - \underline{\hspace{2cm}} = 4,041$

Picking Pairs

ESTIMATE each answer by rounding to the nearest thousand. DRAW a line to connect each problem with the correct estimate of the sum or difference.

4,138 + 2,937 =

7,000

5,701 – 3,639 =

7,642 + 1,426 =

2,000

8,824 – 4,583 =

5,000

6,000

9,000

3,399 + 2,051 =

4,000

9,267 – 2,862 =

Hidden Design

ESTIMATE each answer by rounding to the nearest thousand. Then COLOR the squares that match the numbers to see the hidden design.

4,351 + 2,649 =

9,023 − 4,925 =

1,429 + 1,677 =

8,712 − 8,258 =

3,765 + 1,382 =

9,346 − 2,944 =

5,572 + 3,209 =

7,497 − 4,513 =

7,000	4,000	6,000	1,000	1,000	6,000	4,000	7,000
3,000	7,000	4,000	6,000	6,000	4,000	7,000	3,000
9,000	3,000	7,000	4,000	4,000	7,000	3,000	9,000
5,000	9,000	3,000	2,000	2,000	3,000	9,000	5,000
5,000	9,000	3,000	2,000	2,000	3,000	9,000	5,000
9,000	3,000	7,000	4,000	4,000	7,000	3,000	9,000
3,000	7,000	4,000	6,000	6,000	4,000	7,000	3,000
7,000	4,000	6,000	1,000	1,000	6,000	4,000	7,000

Skate Park

FIND each kind of skateboard in the picture. WRITE the number of groups of each kind of skateboard that can be made.

1. Groups of four skateboards ___4___

2. Groups of two skateboards with animals _____

3. Groups of two skateboards with blue wheels _____

4. Groups of three skateboards with stripes _____

5. Groups of four skateboards with red wheels _____

6. Groups of three skateboards with flames _____

Sandy Shore

DRAW three straight lines in the sand to create six equal sets of shells.

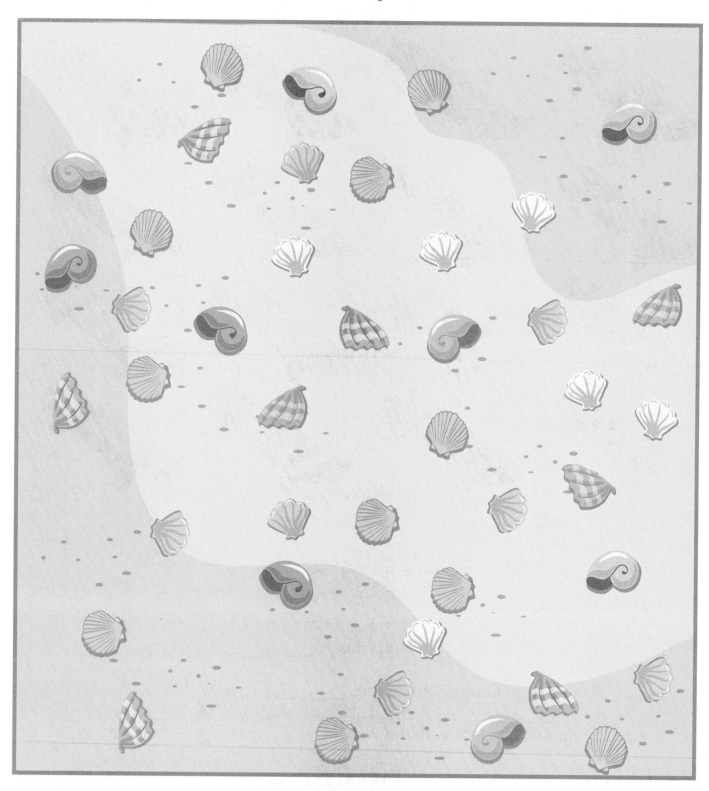

Code Breaker

SOLVE each problem. WRITE the letter that matches each product to solve the riddle.

7	9	4	5	10	8
× 3	× 6	× 2	× 8	× 1	× 6
1	2	3	4	5	6
H	S	I	C	T	D

3	9	6	10	7
× 0	× 7	× 2	× 5	× 4
7	8	9	10	11
P	A	U	R	O

How is a grocery store like a multiplication table?

___ ___ ___ ___ ___
8   10   21   63   54

___ ___ ___ ___ ___ ___ ___ ___.
0   50   28   48   12   40   10   54

Multiplying

Mystery Picture

COLOR each section according to the products to reveal the mystery picture.

8 × 9 =   4 × 6 =   10 × 3 =   5 × 5 =   2 × 8 =   9 × 6 =   7 × 5 =

Pipe Down

WRITE the missing number. Then FOLLOW the pipe, and WRITE the same number in the next problem.

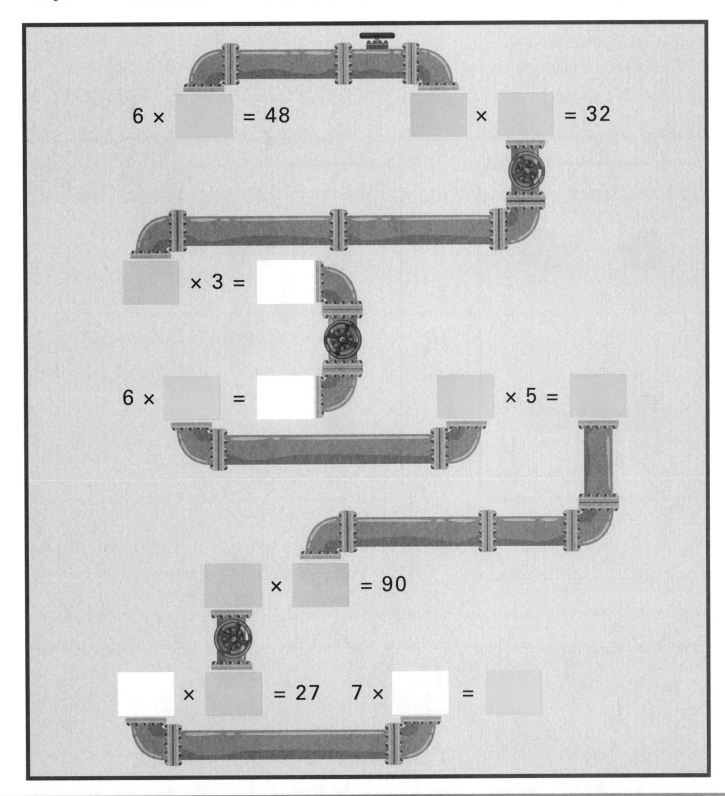

Product Panic

Use the number cards 2 through 10 from a deck of playing cards. READ the rules. PLAY the game!

Rules: Two players
1. Deal all of the cards so both players have an equal stack of cards.
2. Both players flip cards over at the same time.
3. The first player to correctly shout out the product of the two numbers gets to keep the cards.

The player with the most cards at the end of the game wins!

Example:

Bean Counter

Use the beans from page 199, and SHARE them equally among the bowls. START with the number of beans listed, then WRITE how many beans will be in each bowl when the beans are shared equally. (Save the beans to use again later in the workbook.)

1. 15 beans : _____ per bowl

2. 30 beans: _____ per bowl

3. 35 beans: _____ per bowl

4. 45 beans: _____ per bowl

5. 40 beans: _____ per bowl

6. 50 beans: _____ per bowl

Going Bananas

The monkeys want bananas! DRAW a line from each monkey at the top to his basket at the bottom to collect the bananas. You can only cross each banana once, you must cross every banana, and the monkeys must each end up with the same number of bananas. WRITE the number of bananas each monkey has at the end.

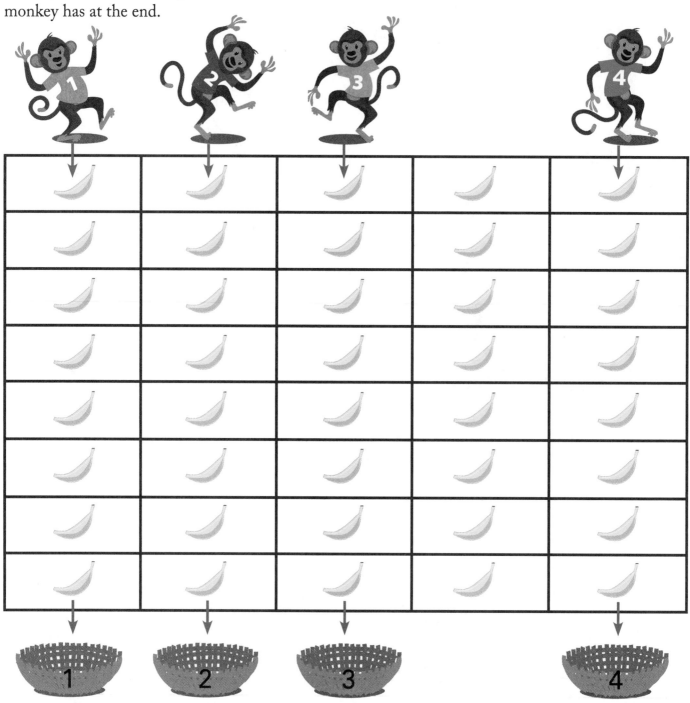

Each monkey gets _____ bananas.

Code Breaker

SOLVE each problem. WRITE the letter that matches each quotient to solve the riddle.

W
1
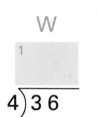
$4\overline{)36}$

T
2
$2\overline{)14}$

O
3
$9\overline{)9}$

C
4
$7\overline{)28}$

A
5
$10\overline{)20}$

R
6
$6\overline{)30}$

U
7
$5\overline{)50}$

H
8
$8\overline{)64}$

I
9
$9\overline{)27}$

L
10
$4\overline{)24}$

$45 \div 9 = ?$

How does a cow do division?

| 9 | 3 | 7 | 8 | | 2 | |

| 4 | 1 | 9 | 4 | 10 | 6 | 2 | 7 | 1 | 5 |

Mystery Picture

COLOR each section according to the quotients to reveal the mystery picture.

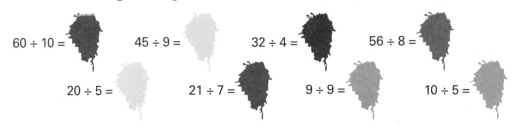

$60 \div 10 =$ $45 \div 9 =$ $32 \div 4 =$ $56 \div 8 =$

$20 \div 5 =$ $21 \div 7 =$ $9 \div 9 =$ $10 \div 5 =$

Pipe Down

WRITE the missing number. Then FOLLOW the pipe, and WRITE the same number in the next problem.

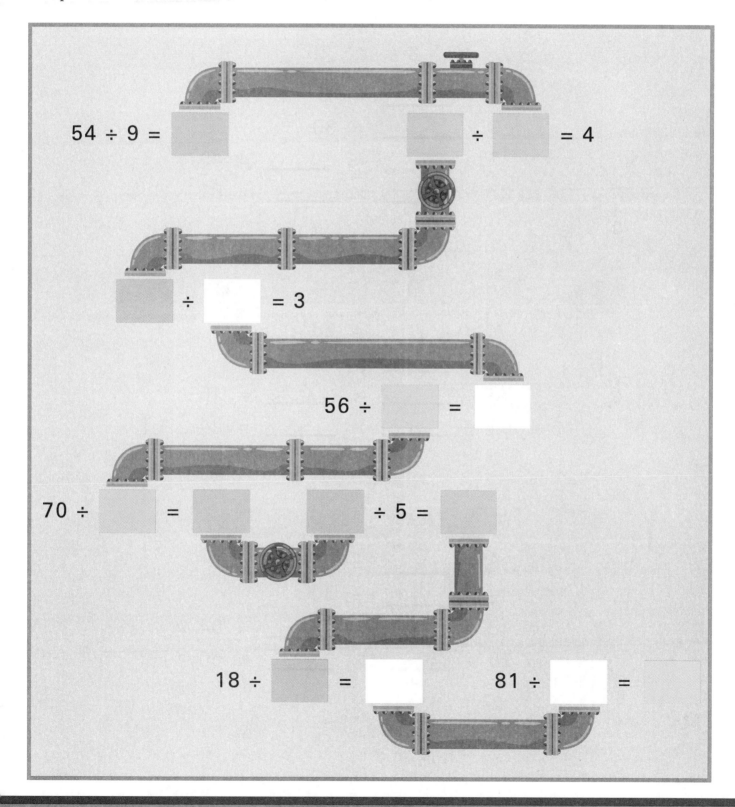

$54 \div 9 = \boxed{}$ $\boxed{} \div \boxed{} = 4$

$\boxed{} \div \boxed{} = 3$

$56 \div \boxed{} = \boxed{}$

$70 \div \boxed{} = \boxed{} \div 5 = \boxed{}$

$18 \div \boxed{} = \boxed{}$ $81 \div \boxed{} = \boxed{}$

Number Nudge

For each set of problems, WRITE the missing numbers so that the answers are correct.

1	7	3	10	9	6

1. $54 \div \underline{\hspace{1cm}} = 9$
2. $3 \times \underline{\hspace{1cm}} = 30$
3. $7 \div \underline{\hspace{1cm}} \times \underline{\hspace{1cm}} = 49$
4. $27 \div \underline{\hspace{1cm}} \times \underline{\hspace{1cm}} = 81$

2	7	3	4	8	5

5. $7 \times \underline{\hspace{1cm}} = 28$
6. $35 \div \underline{\hspace{1cm}} = 7$
7. $56 \div \underline{\hspace{1cm}} \times \underline{\hspace{1cm}} = 16$
8. $64 \div \underline{\hspace{1cm}} \times \underline{\hspace{1cm}} = 24$

9	6	4	2	8	5

9. $36 \div \underline{\hspace{1cm}} = 9$
10. $8 \times \underline{\hspace{1cm}} = 40$
11. $48 \div \underline{\hspace{1cm}} \times \underline{\hspace{1cm}} = 54$
12. $20 \div \underline{\hspace{1cm}} \times \underline{\hspace{1cm}} = 60$

Skipping Stones

DRAW a path through all of the factors of 24 to cross the river.

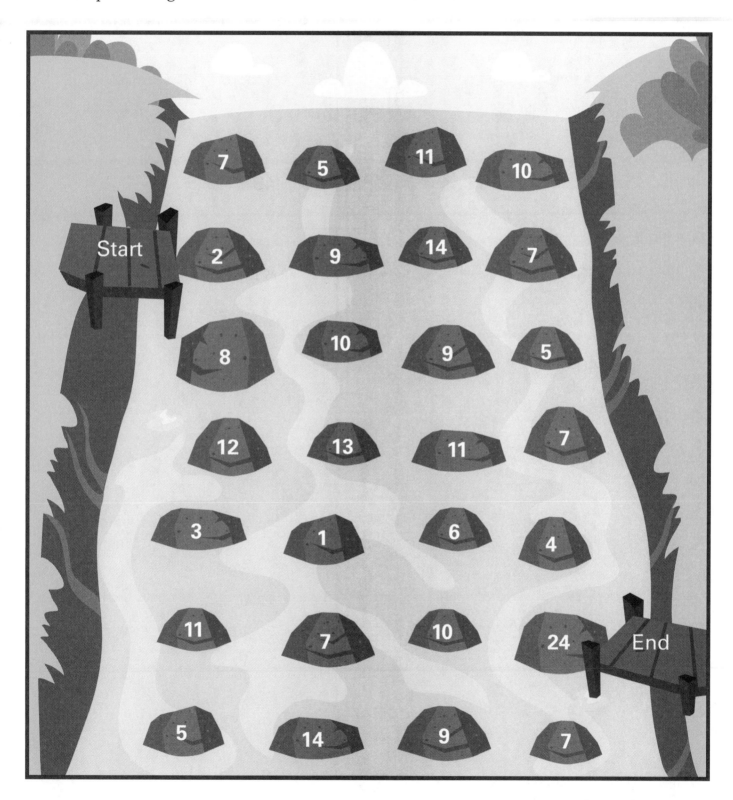

Just Right

WRITE each number so that it is a factor of the blue number.

HINT: There may be more than one place to put a number, but you need to use every factor!

| 5 | 9 | 6 | 3 | 8 | 4 | 10 | 7 |

42 _____
1

49 _____
2

36 _____
3

81 _____
4

40 _____
5

25 _____
6

16 _____
7

3 _____
8

Multiple Maze

DRAW a line to get from the start of the maze to the end, crossing through only multiples of 8.

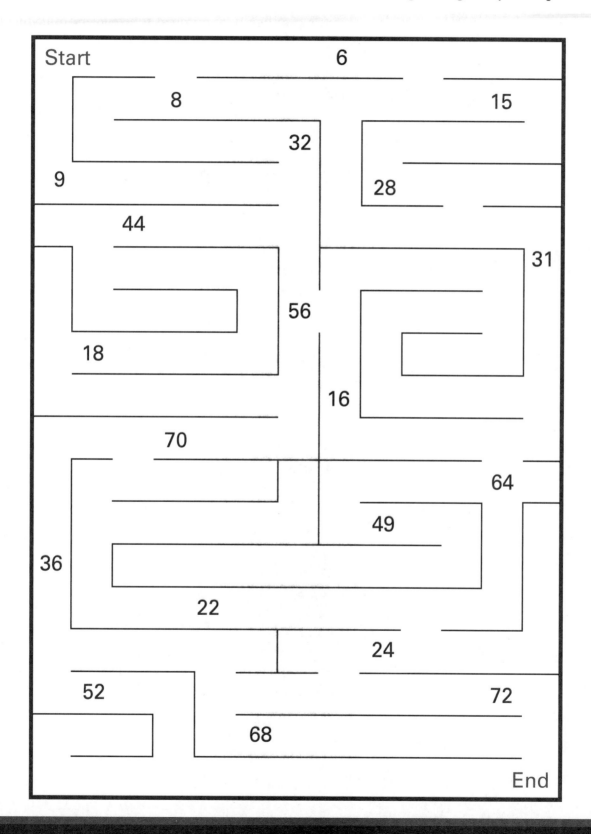

Start
6
8
15
32
9
28
44
31
56
18
16
70
64
49
36
22
24
52
72
68
End

Just Right

WRITE each number so that it is a multiple of the blue number.

HINT: There may be more than one place to put a number, but you need to use every multiple!

15	3	48	64	4	35	18	50

4

1

9

2

6

3

3

4

10

5

8

6

5

7

7

8

Uniform Central

READ the paragraph, and WRITE the answer.

The Callicoon Clippers need new hockey uniforms. The team can choose from five different hockey jerseys and three different kinds of pants. How many different uniforms can be made from these options?

_____ uniforms

Sandwich Stackers

READ the paragraph, and WRITE the answer.

There are three different kinds of bread, three different kinds of meat, and two different kinds of cheese. If each sandwich is made with one kind of bread, one kind of meat, and one kind of cheese, how many different sandwiches can be made?

_____ sandwiches

Who Sits Where?

WRITE the name of each person on the correct seat.

Erik likes a window seat.

Alana doesn't want to sit next to Tyler or Mia.

Tyler gets cold easily and won't sit next to the window.

Oscar and Tyler like to sit next to each other.

Mia always sits closest to the jukebox.

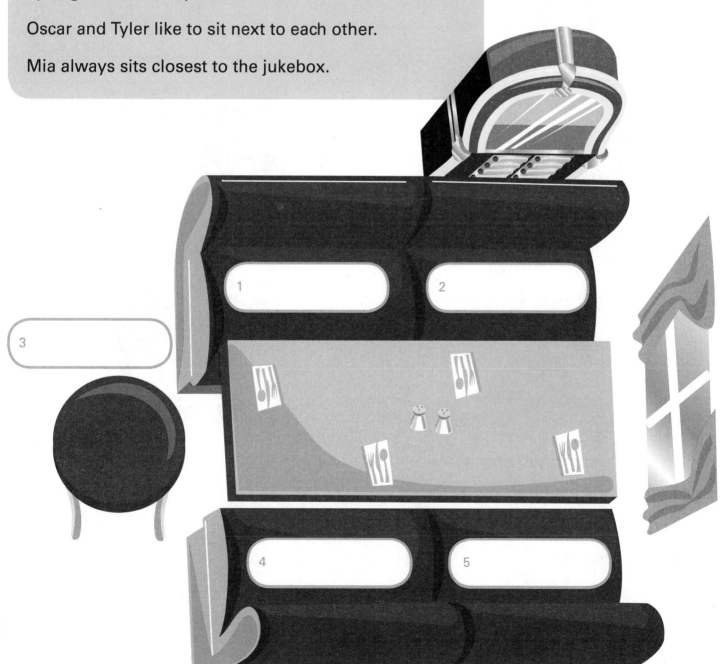

Frozen Dinner Night

WRITE the name of each person below the correct meal.

1

2

3

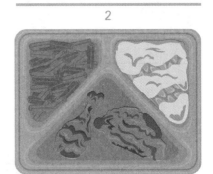

4

5

6

Jayden doesn't eat meat.

Sara loves fried chicken but hates corn.

Sharon wants pasta.

Adam won't eat if there's anything green on his plate.

Patrick loves meatloaf.

Jayden and TJ don't get dessert with their meal.

Totally Tangled

FIND the fraction and picture pairs that are connected, and COLOR any fraction that does **not** match the picture.

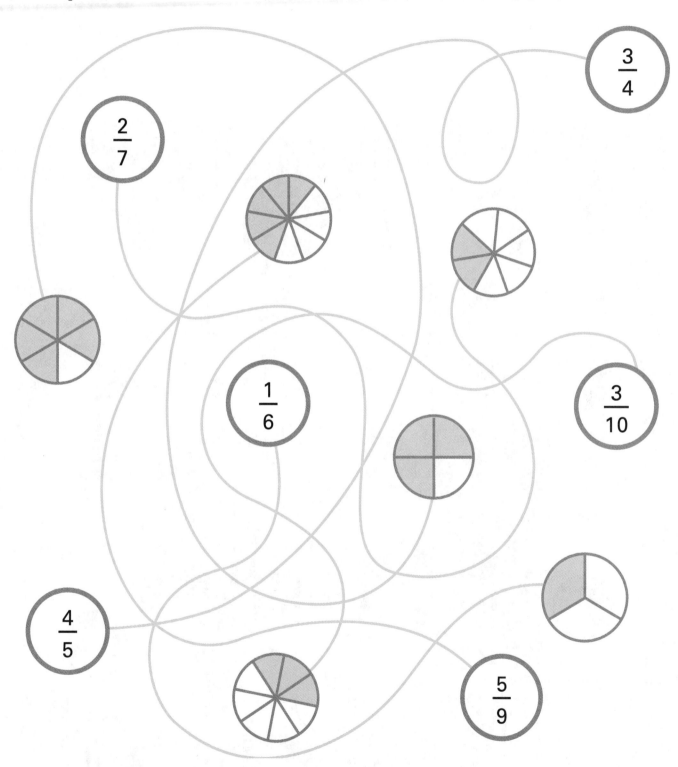

Garden Trail

Can you be the first to reach the end? Use two small objects as playing pieces and the spinner from page 201. READ the rules. PLAY the game!

(Save the spinner to use again later in the workbook.)

Rules: Two players
1. Place the playing pieces at START.
2. Take turns spinning the spinner. Move ahead to the closest fraction picture that matches the fraction on the spinner.
3. If you land on a tree stump, you lose a turn.

The first player to get through the garden trail wins!

What's the Password?

WRITE the letters that form a fraction of each word. Then WRITE the letters in order to find the secret password.

1. The first $\frac{1}{7}$ of RAINBOW _____

2. The first $\frac{2}{5}$ of OLIVE _____

3. The last $\frac{1}{2}$ of HOLE _____

4. The middle $\frac{1}{3}$ of ART _____

5. The first $\frac{2}{6}$ of COPPER _____

6. The last $\frac{3}{4}$ of FAST _____

7. The last $\frac{2}{7}$ of PAINTER _____

Password:

_____ _____ _____ _____ _____ _____

_____ _____ _____ _____ _____ _____

Flower Power

Use the spinner from page 201. SPIN the spinner, and WRITE the fraction on a flower. DRAW and COLOR petals on the flower to match the fraction. COLOR the rest of the petals another color. (Save the spinner to use again.)

Example:

$\frac{2}{7}$ of the petals are red.

Fraction Factory

Can you be the first to reach the end? Use two small objects as playing pieces and the spinner from page 202. READ the rules. PLAY the game!

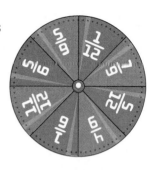

Rules: Two players

1. Place the playing pieces at Start.
2. Take turns spinning the spinner. Move ahead to the closest fraction picture that matches the fraction on the spinner. Fractions are shown by the fraction of muffins filling the muffin tin.
3. If you land on a red muffin tin, you get to spin again.

The first player to get boxed up wins!

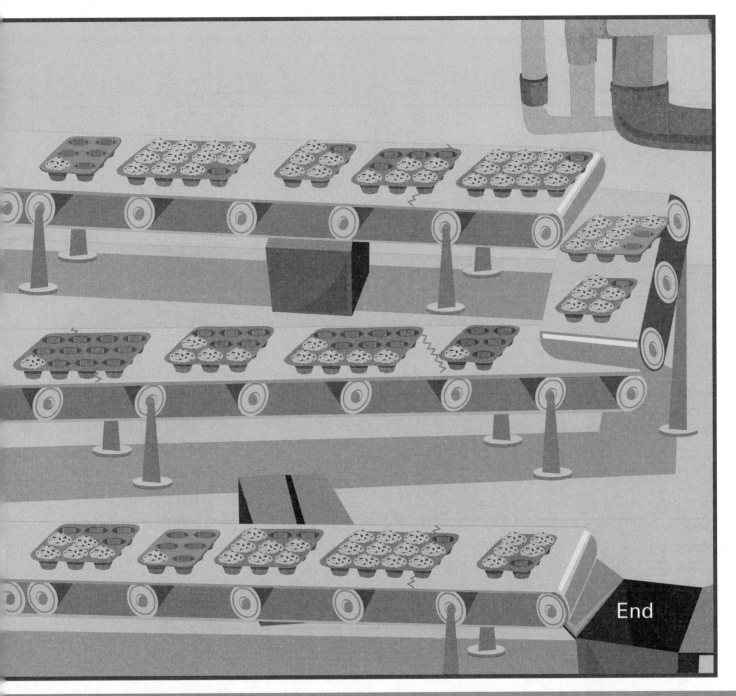

Code Breaker

WRITE the fraction for each picture. WRITE the letter that matches each fraction to solve the riddle.

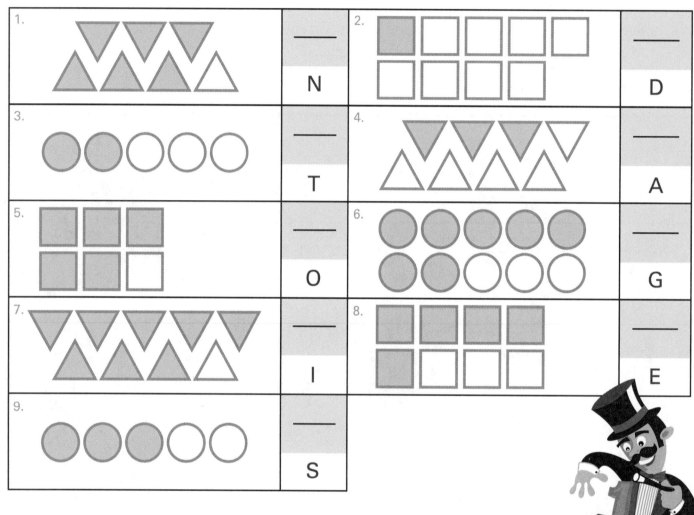

How do you make one disappear?

$$\frac{3}{8} \quad \frac{1}{9} \quad \frac{1}{9} \qquad \frac{3}{8} \qquad \frac{7}{10} \qquad \frac{3}{8} \quad \frac{6}{7} \quad \frac{1}{9}$$

,

$$\frac{8}{9} \quad \frac{2}{5} \quad \frac{3}{5} \qquad \frac{7}{10} \quad \frac{5}{6} \quad \frac{6}{7} \quad \frac{5}{8}.$$

Totally Tangled

Each fraction is connected to a picture. FIND the pairs of fractions, and COLOR any fraction that is smaller than the picture it is connected to.

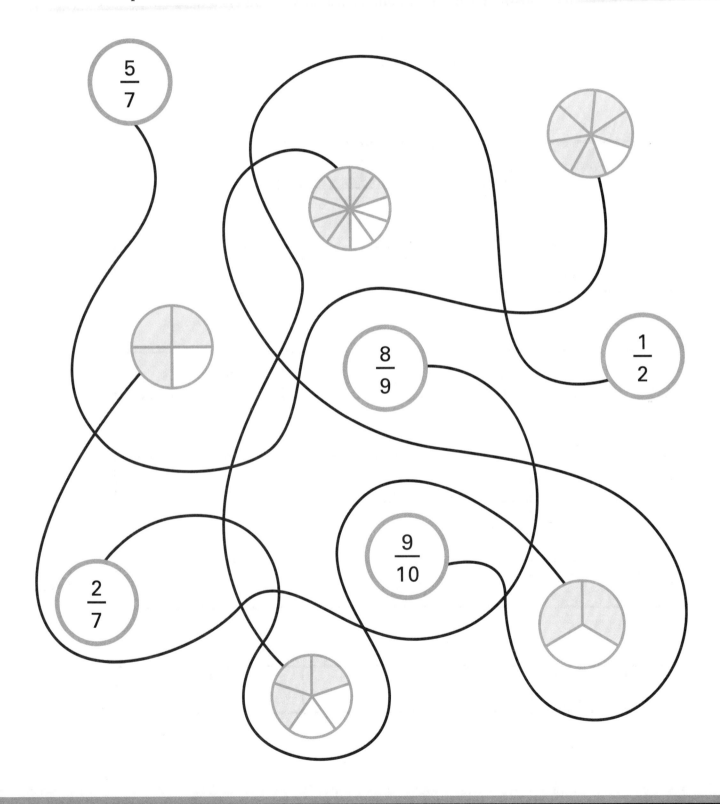

Just Right

WRITE each fraction next to a smaller fraction.

HINT: There may be more than one place to put a fraction, but you need to use every fraction!

$$\frac{4}{6} \quad \frac{1}{3} \quad \frac{5}{6} \quad \frac{1}{2} \quad \frac{8}{9} \quad \frac{1}{8}$$

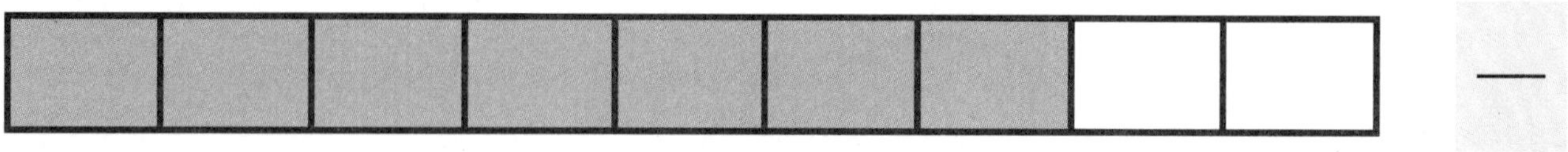

1

2

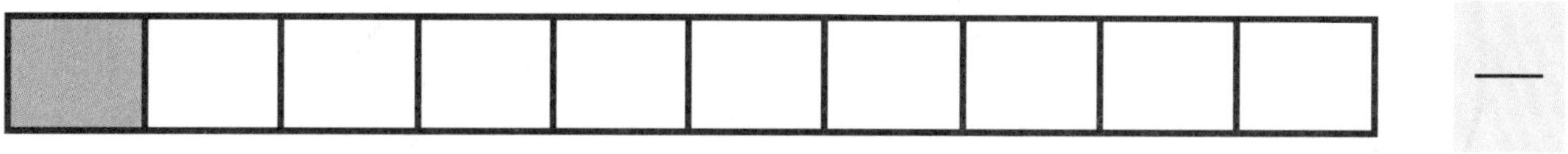

3

4

5

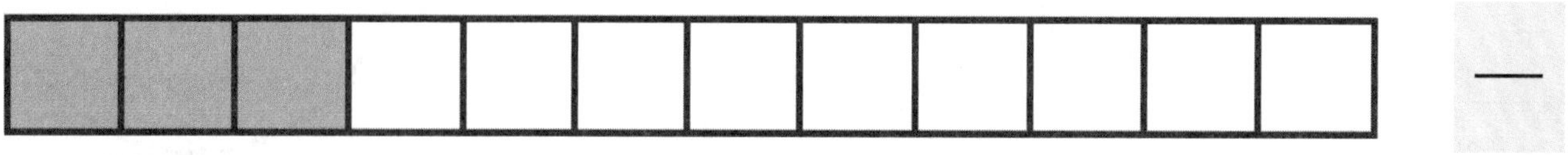

6

Code Ruler

WRITE the letter that appears at each measurement to answer the riddle.

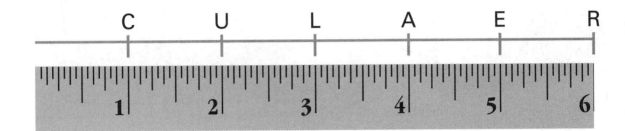

C U L A E R

1 2 3 4 5 6

What has a foot but can't hop?

___ ___ ___ ___ ___ ___.
4 in. 6 in. 2 in. 3 in. 5 in. 6 in.

Sidewalk Slugs

MEASURE each slug in centimeters. DRAW lines connecting pairs of slugs that are the same length.

Gallon Imposter

Each of the pictures except for one is equal to 1 gallon. DRAW an X on the imposter.

2 cups = 1 pint

2 pints = 1 quart

4 quarts = 1 gallon

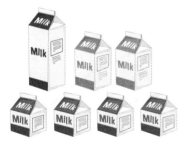

Totally Tangled

FIND the measurements that are connected. COLOR the smaller measurement in each pair.

2 cups (c) = 1 pint (pt)   4 quarts = 1 gallon (gal)

2 pints = 1 quart (qt)   1 liter (L) = 1,000 milliliters (mL)

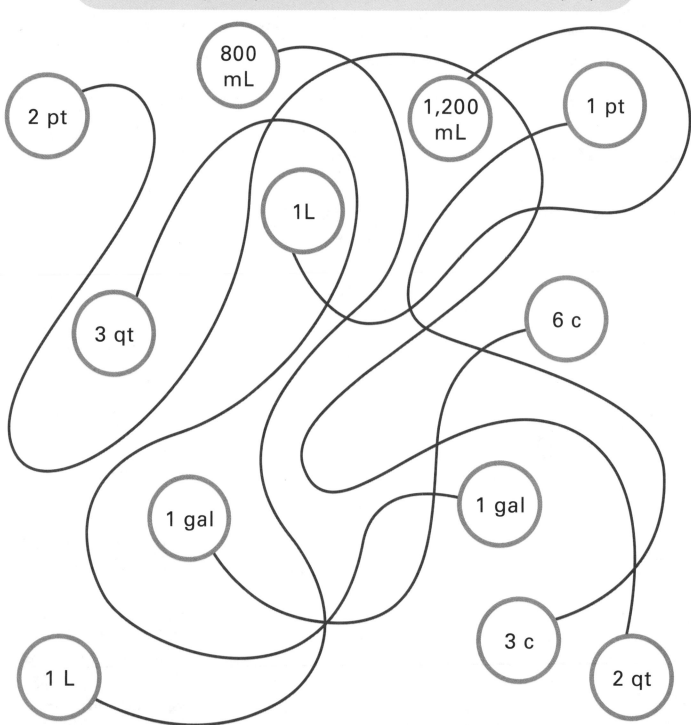

Slide Sort

CIRCLE the measurements that do not match what you would use to measure the object at the bottom of the slide.

1 pound (lb) = 16 ounces (oz)   1 kilogram (kg) = 1,000 grams (g)

pound   kilogram   ounce   gram

Totally Tangled

FIND the measurements that are connected. COLOR the larger measurement in each pair.

1 pound (lb) = 16 ounces (oz)   1 kilogram (kg) = 1,000 grams (g)

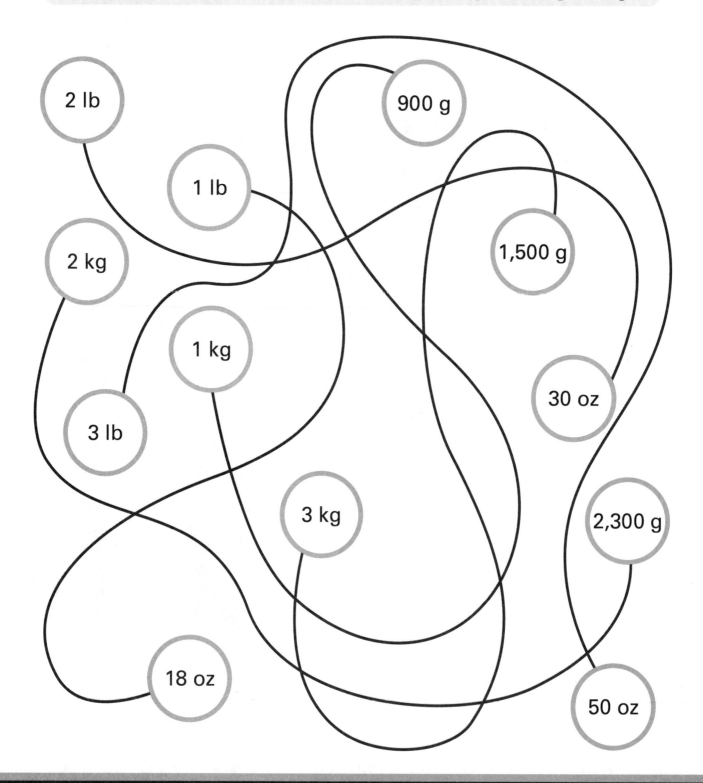

Picking Pairs

DRAW a line to match each thermometer with the right window.

Code Breaker

WRITE the letter that matches each temperature to solve the riddle.

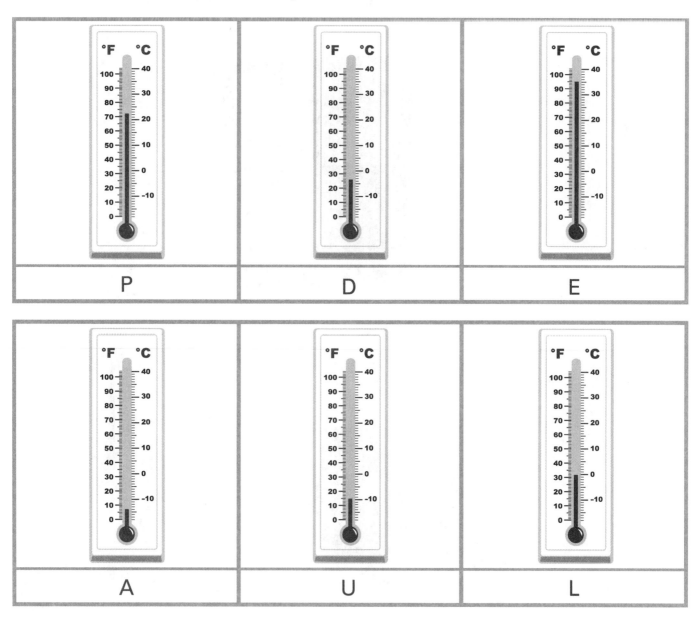

| P | D | E |

| A | U | L |

What do you call a snowman in the summertime?

___ ___ ___ ___ ___ ___ ___.

7°F   72°F   15°F   26°F   26°F   32°F   95°F

Puzzling Pattern

CIRCLE the set of shapes that completes the pattern.

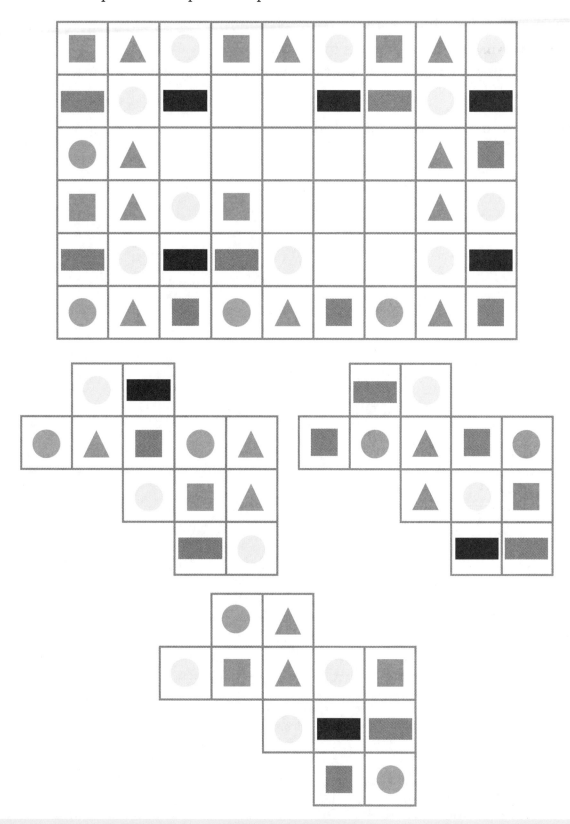

Secure the Square

Can you connect all of the dots to make squares? READ the rules. PLAY the game!

Rules: Two players
1. Take turns drawing one line to connect two dots.
2. If your line forms one or more squares, write your initials in any square you made. If you make a square, take another turn.

The player with the most squares at the end wins!

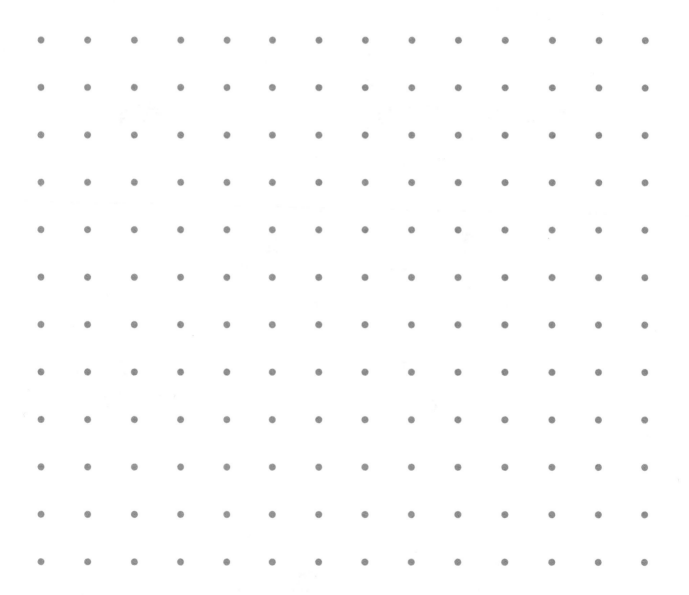

Player 1: _____   Player 2: _____

Three Beans

Use the beans from page 199, and PLACE each bean on a dot. MOVE only three beans to make the triangle point up instead of down.

Trap the Circle

CONNECT the dots to trap the circle in between a square and a hexagon. Do not lift your pencil, and do not trace over any line already drawn.

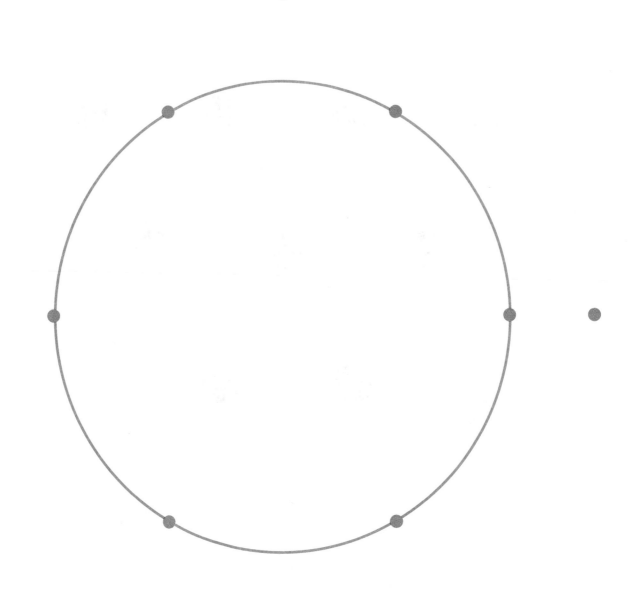

Puzzling Pattern

CIRCLE the set of shapes that completes the pattern.

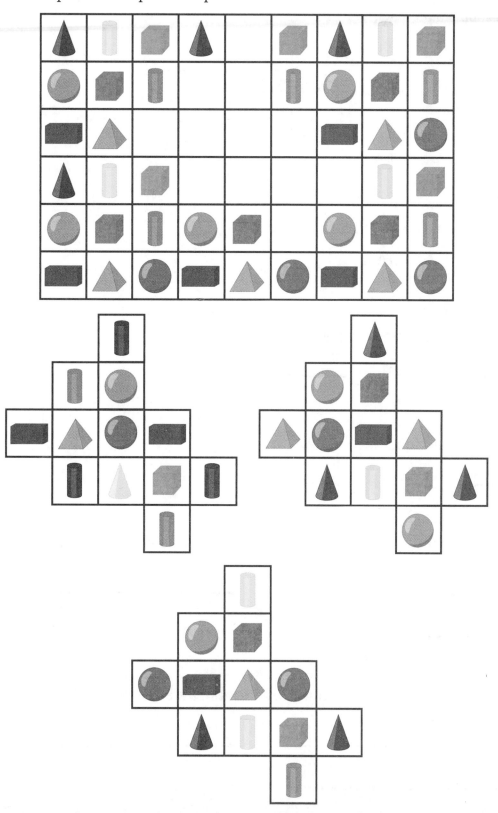

Shape Builders

CUT OUT each shape on the opposite page. FOLD on the dotted lines, and GLUE the tabs to construct each solid shape. Then WRITE the answers to the questions.

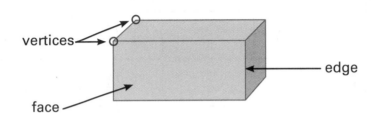

1. How many faces does each shape have?

   Blue: _____   Green: _____

2. How many vertices does each shape have?

   Blue: _____   Green: _____

3. How many edges does each shape have:

   Blue: _____   Green: _____

Write the name of three things in your home that have a shape similar to the blue shape.

_____   _____

_____

Write the name of three things in your home that have a shape similar to the green shape.

_____   _____

_____

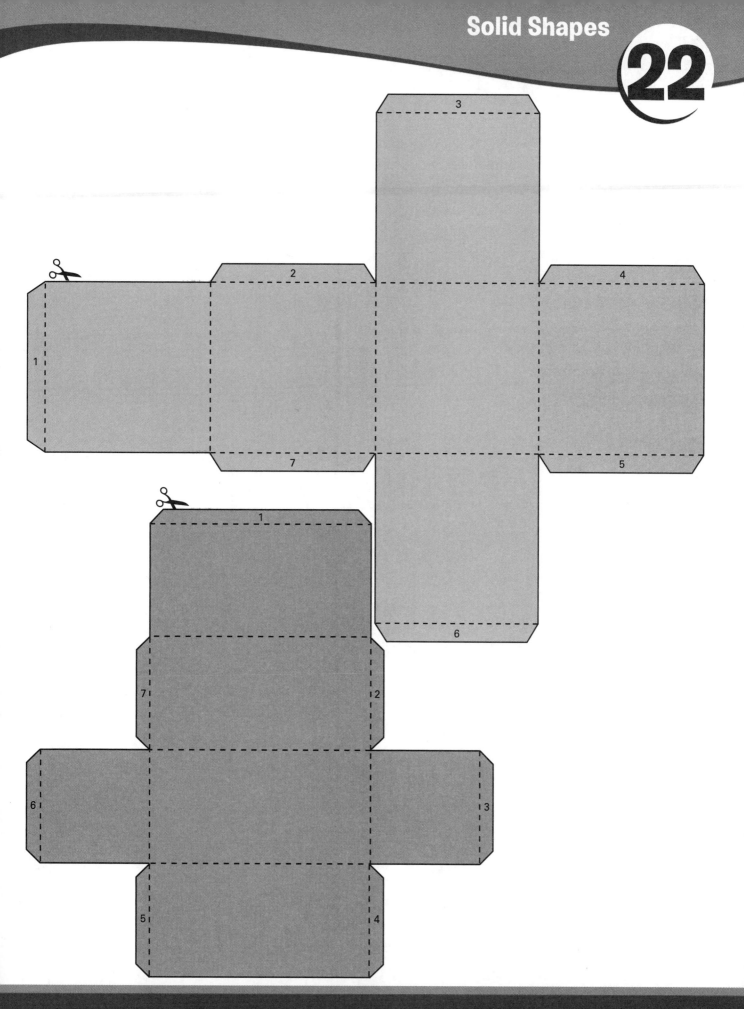

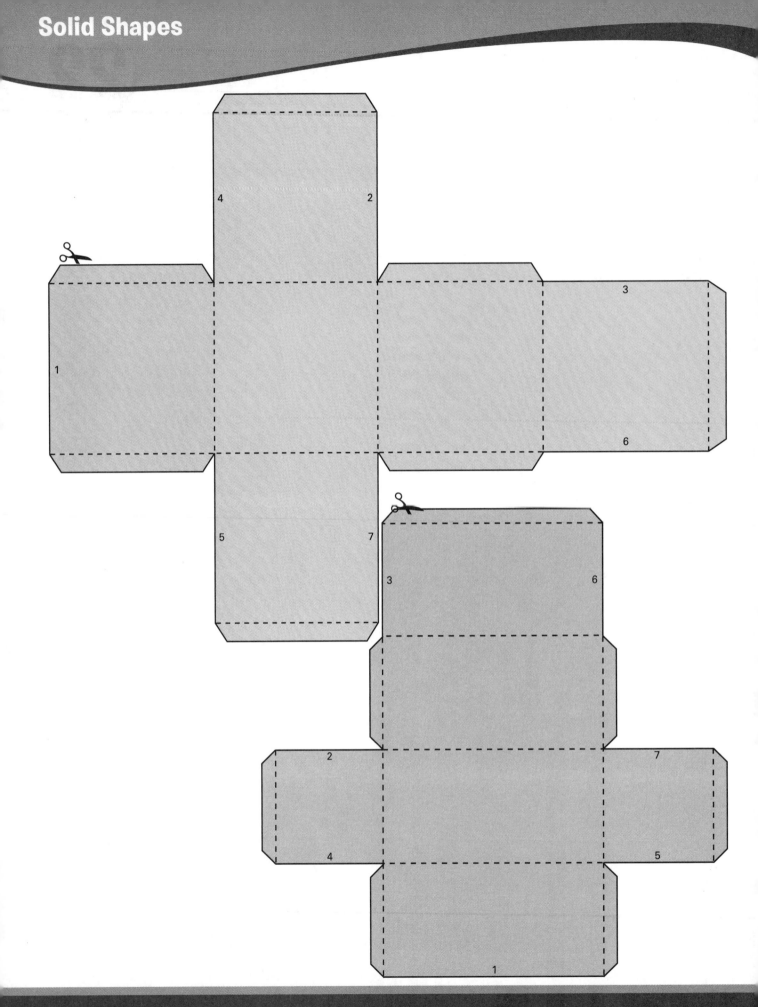

Shape Shifters

A shape has **symmetry** if a line can divide the shape so each half is a mirror image of the other. Use the pattern block pieces from page 203, and PLACE the pieces to make the picture symmetrical. (Save the pattern block pieces to use again later in the workbook.)

Shape Shifters

Use the pattern block pieces from page 203, and PLACE the pieces to make each picture symmetrical. (Save the pattern block pieces to use again.)

Paper Cuts

DRAW the rest of each shape to make it symmetrical, using the dotted line as the line of symmetry. Then CUT OUT each shape. FOLD along the dotted line to see how close your drawing was.

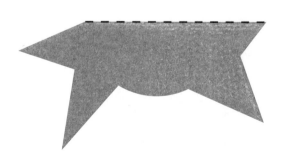

After you finish your drawing on page 183, CUT OUT the entire shape.

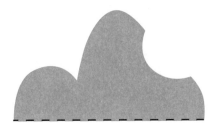

Tricky Tangrams

Use the tangram pieces from page 205, and PLACE the pieces to completely fill each shape without overlapping any pieces. (Save the tangram pieces to use again.)

HINT: Try placing the biggest pieces first.

Tricky Tangrams

Use the tangram pieces from page 205, and PLACE the pieces to completely fill each shape without overlapping any pieces. (Save the tangram pieces to use again.)

HINT: Try placing the biggest pieces first.

Incredible Illusions

A **tessellation** is a repeating pattern of shapes that has no gaps or overlapping shapes. COLOR the rest of the tessellation. Do the yellow shapes look like they're facing up or down?

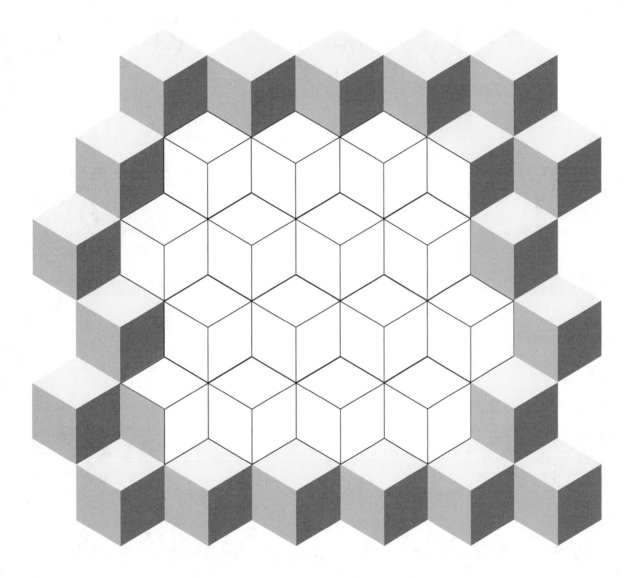

Shape Shifters

Use the pattern block pieces from page 203, and PLACE the pieces to finish the tessellation.

Code Breaker

LOOK at the time shown on each clock. Then WRITE the letter that matches each time to solve the riddle.

| O | A | T | L |

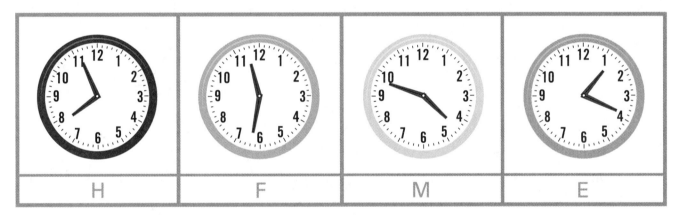

| H | F | M | E |

What months have 28 days?

$\overline{}$ $\overline{}$ $\overline{}$ $\overline{}$ $\overline{}$
10:47   12:04   12:04   3:12   11:32

$\overline{}$ $\overline{}$ $\overline{}$ $\overline{}$.
5:27   7:56   1:19   4:48

Mystery Time

COLOR the times in the picture according to the color of the clocks at the top. When you are done coloring, WRITE the mystery time under the picture

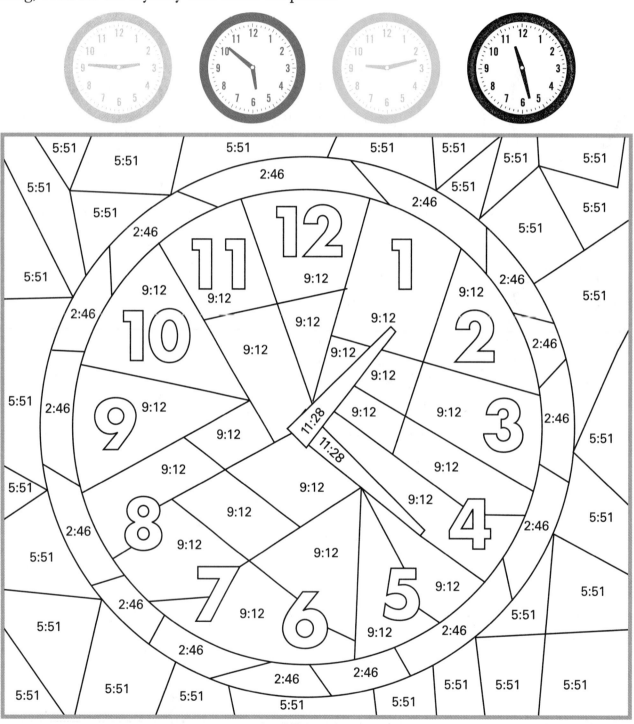

:

Time Travel

DRAW a line from Start through the clocks to get to the end, traveling ahead 1 hour and 8 minutes as you go from clock to clock.

Start

End

Totally Tangled

FIND the time and clock pairs that are connected. COLOR any time that is **not** 4 hours and 26 minutes away from the time shown on the clock.

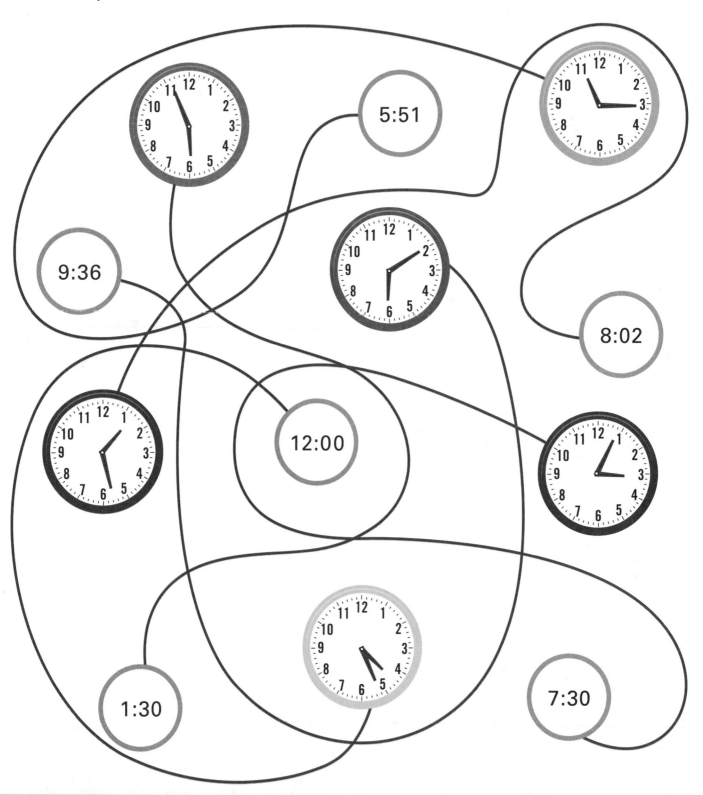

Time Travel

DRAW a line from Start through the clocks to get to the end, traveling backward 2 hours and 33 minutes as you go from clock to clock.

Start

End

Who Am I?

READ the clues, and CIRCLE the mystery time.

HINT: Cross out any time that does not match the clues.

I am between the hours of 3:00 and 10:00.

I am 1 hour and 42 minutes later than another clock on stage.

I am 2 hours and 3 minutes earlier than another clock on stage.

Who am I?

Pocket Change

DRAW two straight lines to create four different money sets of equal value.

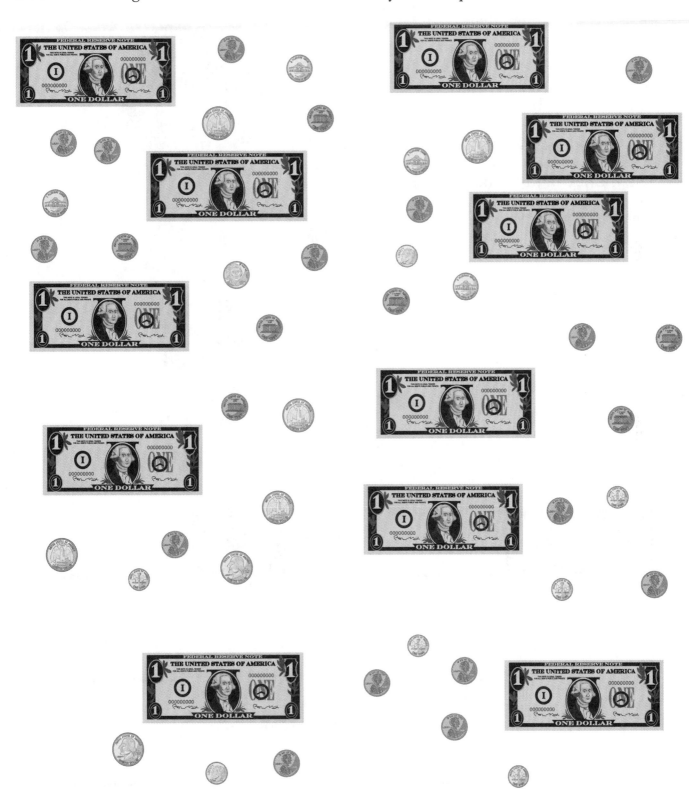

What's in My Hand?

READ the clues and WRITE the number of each coin and bill hidden in the hand.

I'm holding three paper bills and six coins.

The money in my hand totals $7.46.

I don't have any quarters.

What's in my hand?

_____
1

_____
2

_____
3

_____
4

_____
5

_____
6

Pocket Change

DRAW three straight lines to create six different money sets of equal value.

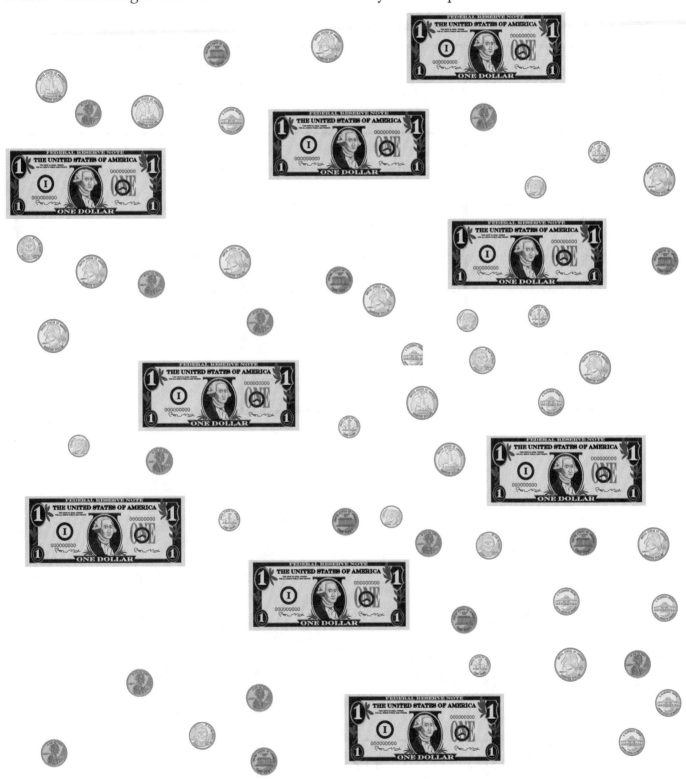

Code Breaker

SOLVE each problem. WRITE the letter that matches each dollar amount to solve the riddle.

$3.00 \times 5 = $ ____ 1	$16.00 \div 4 = $ ____ 2	$2.00 \times 3 = $ ____ 3
E	F	T
$12.00 \div 6 = $ ____ 4	$5.00 \div 2 = $ ____ 5	$1.25 \times 3 = $ ____ 6
V	N	C
$7.00 \div 4 = $ ____ 7	$2.50 \times 5 = $ ____ 8	
I	S	

What's the difference between
a new dime and an old nickel?

____ ____ ____ ____
$4.00 $1.75 $2.00 $15.00

____ ____ ____ ____ ____ .
$3.75 $15.00 $2.50 $6.00 $12.50

Beans

CUT OUT the beans.

These beans are for use with pages 141 and 175.

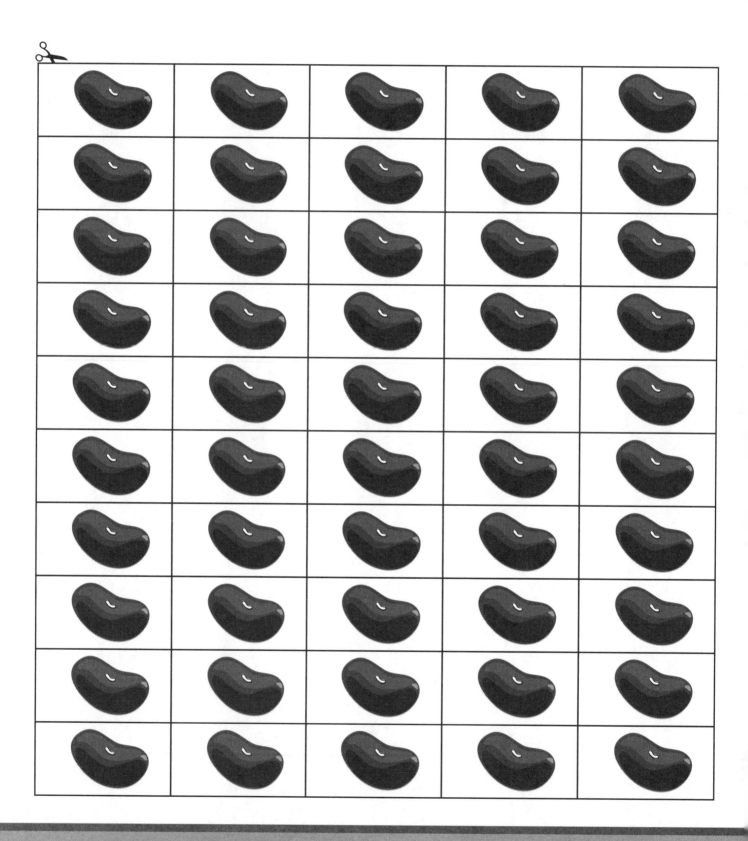

Spinners

CUT OUT the spinner. BEND the outer part of a paper clip so that it points out, and carefully POKE it through the center dot of the spinner. You're ready to spin!

This spinner is for use with pages 156, 157, and 159. The spinner on the reverse side is for use with pages 160 and 161.

Use the spinner on this side for pages 160 and 161. Pull out the paper clip from the other side, and poke it through the center dot on this side.

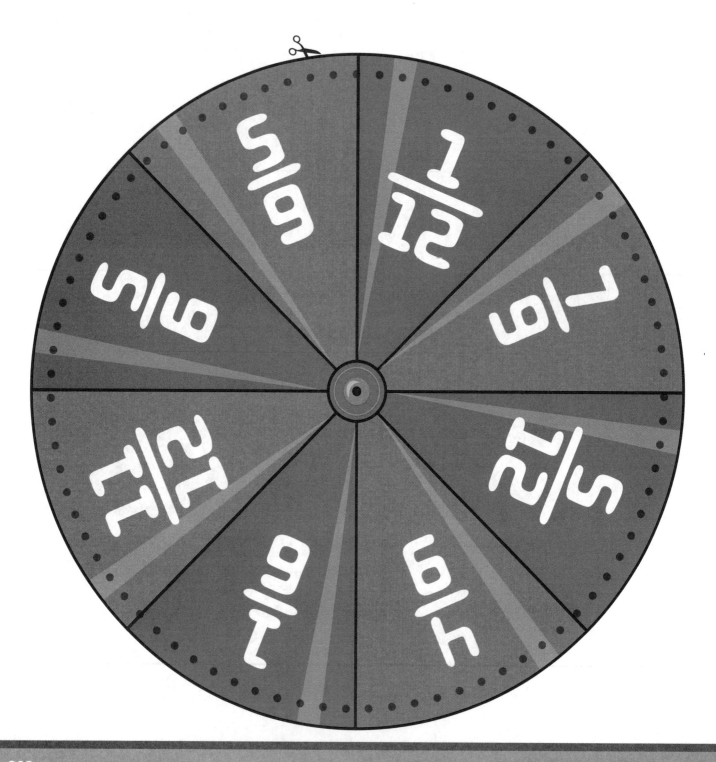

Pattern Blocks

CUT OUT the 31 pattern block pieces.

These pattern block pieces are for use with pages 181, 182, and 188.

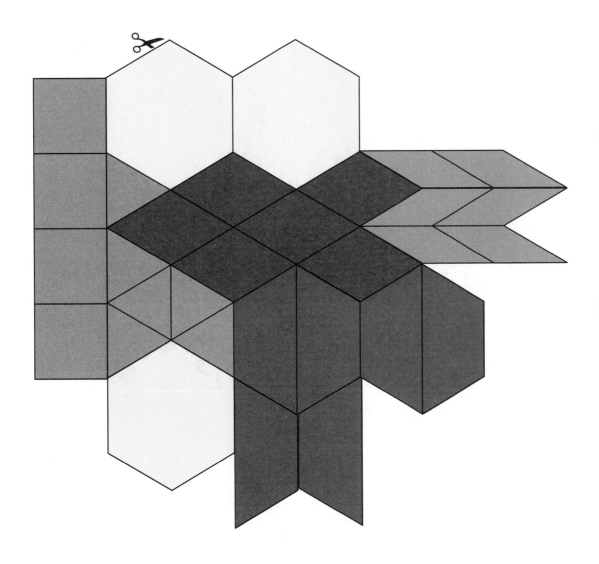

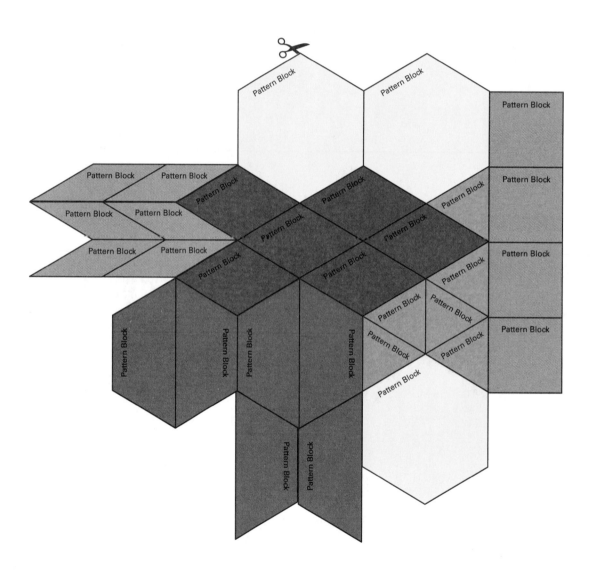

Pattern Block

Tangrams

CUT OUT the seven tangram pieces.

These tangram pieces are for use with pages 185 and 186.

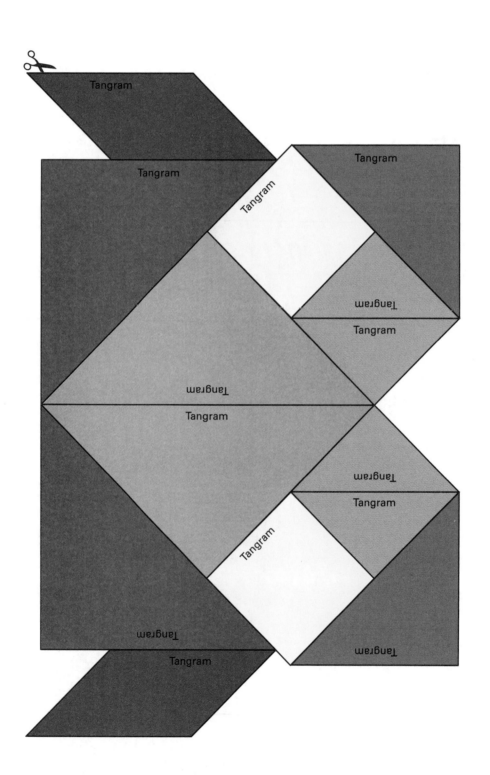

Page 105
1. 1,283 2. 4,565 3. 2,419
4. 7,332 5. 5,817
Combination: 1 2 4 5 7

Pages 106–107
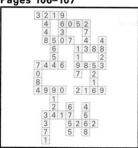

Page 108
1. 7,626 2. 4,155 3. 8,303
4. 1,984 5. 6,497 6. 2,849
7. 5,224

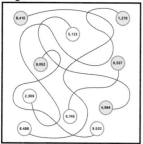

Page 109
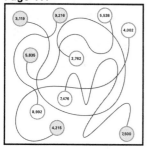

Page 110

Page 111

Page 112
1,368	1,386	1,638	1,683
1,836	1,863	3,168	3,186
3,618	3,681	3,816	3,861
6,138	6,183	6,318	6,381
6,813	6,831	8,136	8,163
8,316	8,361	8,613	8,631

Page 113
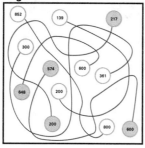

Page 114
1. 5,755   2. 4,372
3. 5,845   4. 4,498
5. 5,178   6. 5,136
7. 5,742   8. 4,375
9. 5,213

Page 116
Check: 119

Page 117
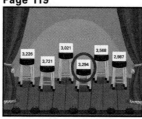

Page 118
1. 245, 266
2. 140, 230
3. 264, 300
Combination:
140 230 245 264 266 300

Page 119

Page 120
5,674

Page 121
1. 43   2. 22   3. 51
4. 36   5. 65   6. 17

Page 122
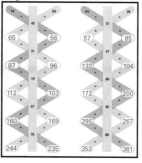

Page 123
58	+	92	=	150
+		+		+
134	+	249	=	383
=		=		=
192	+	341	=	533

Page 124
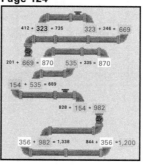

Page 125
1. 7,228   2. 1,262
3. 5,950   4. 3,843
5. 3,394   6. 8,636
7. 5,492   8. 2,530
9. 8,762   10. 9,917
11. 9,256   12. 6,398
It's a FRIEND YOU CAN
COUNT ON.

Page 126
1. 1,728
2. 2,037
3. 1,410, 3,185
4. 2,959
5. 2,541
6. 1,588, 3,218
7. 1,188
8. 1,549
9. 1,713, 1,236

Page 127
1. 12   2. 62   3. 34
4. 49   5. 55   6. 28

Page 128
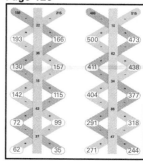

Page 129
492	−	179	=	313
−		−		−
261	−	47	=	214
=		=		=
231	−	132	=	99

Page 130
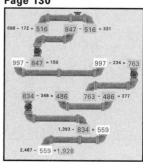

Page 131
1. 3,897   2. 2,156
3. 7,982   4. 5,294
5. 5,853   6. 7,689
7. 3,477   8. 4,586
9. 5,379   10. 4,366
11. 6,170   12. 1,237
SUBTRACT THE I AND E.

Page 132
1. 992
2. 3,123
3. 1,014, 1,258
4. 2,367
5. 2,004
6. 1,702, 2,591
7. 3,289
8. 4,330
9. 1,542, 3,921

Answers

Page 133

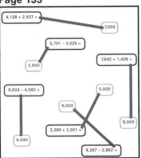

Page 134

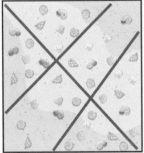

Page 135

1. 4   2. 2   3. 5
4. 3   5. 1   6. 2

Page 136

Page 137

1. 21   2. 54   3. 8
4. 40   5. 10   6. 48
7. 0   8. 63   9. 12
10. 50 11. 28
IT HAS PRODUCTS.

Page 138

Page 139

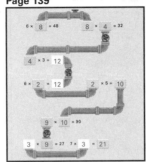

Page 140

Have someone check your
answers.

Page 141

1. 3   2. 6   3. 7
4. 9   5. 8   6. 10

Page 142

Suggestion:

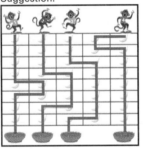

10

Page 143

1. 9   2 7   3. 1
4. 4   5. 2   6. 5
7. 10 8. 8   9. 3
10. 6
WITH A COWCULATOR.

Page 144

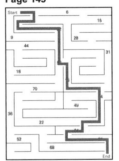

Page 145

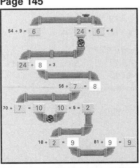

Page 146

1. 6   2. 10   3. 1, 7
4. 3, 9 5. 4   6. 5
7. 7, 2 8. 8, 3 9. 4
10. 5   11. 8, 9 12. 2, 6

Page 147

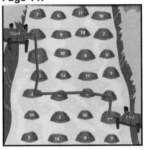

Page 148

1. 6   2. 7   3. 4
4. 9   5. 10 6. 5
7. 8   8. 3

Page 149

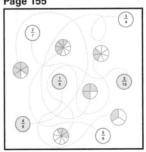

Page 150

1. 4   2. 18 3. 48
4. 3   5. 50 6. 64
7. 15 8. 35

Page 151

15

Page 152

18

Page 153

1. Tyler   2. Mia   3. Oscar
4. Alana   5. Erik

Page 154

1. Adam   2. Sharon
3. TJ   4. Sara
5. Jayden 6. Patrick

Page 155

Pages 156–157

Have someone check your
answers.

Page 158

1. R   2. OL   3. LE
4. R   5. CO   6. AST
7. ER
ROLLER COASTER

Page 159

Have someone check your
answers.

Pages 160–161

Have someone check your
answers.

Page 162

1. $\frac{6}{7}$ 2. $\frac{1}{9}$

3. $\frac{2}{5}$ 4. $\frac{3}{8}$

5. $\frac{5}{6}$ 6. $\frac{7}{10}$

7. $\frac{8}{9}$ 8. $\frac{5}{8}$

9. $\frac{3}{5}$

ADD A G AND IT'S GONE.

Page 163

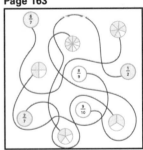

Page 164

1. $\frac{8}{9}$ 2. $\frac{5}{6}$ 3. $\frac{1}{8}$

4. $\frac{1}{2}$ 5. $\frac{4}{6}$ 6. $\frac{1}{3}$

Page 165

A RULER.

Page 166

Page 167

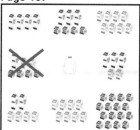

Page 168

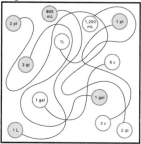

Page 169
pound, gram

Page 170

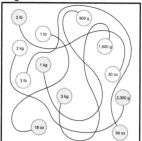

Page 171

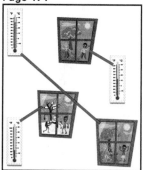

Page 172
A PUDDLE.

Page 173

Page 174
Have someone check
your answers.

Page 175
Suggestion:

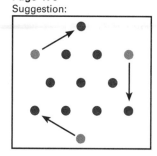

Page 176
First connect the six dots on the
circle to make a hexagon.

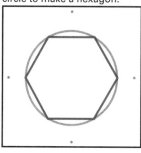

Then connect the last dot of the
hexagon to a dot on the outside
of the circle.

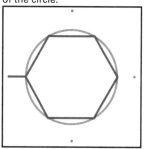

Finally, draw a square around
the circle.

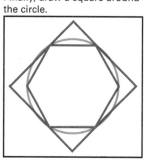

Page 177

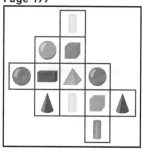

Page 178
1. 6, 6   2. 8, 8   3. 12, 12
Have someone check
your answers.

Page 181

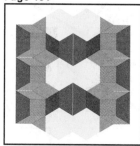

Page 182

Page 183

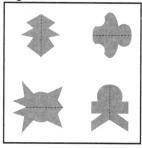

Page 185
Suggestion:

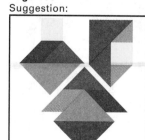

Page 186
Suggestion:

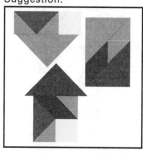

Page 187

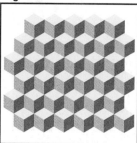

Page 188

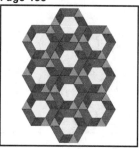

Page 189
ALL OF THEM.

Answers

Page 190

1:22

Page 191

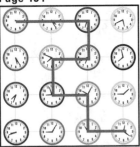

Page 192

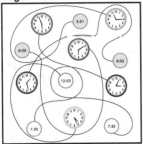

Page 193

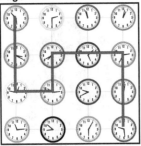

Page 194

Page 195

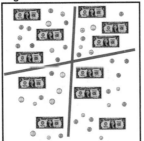

Page 196

1. 1	2. 2	3. 0
4. 4	5. 1	6. 1

Page 197

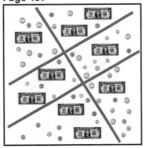

Page 198

1. $15.00	2. $4.00
3. $6.00	4 $2.00
5. $2.50	6. $3.75
7. $1.75	8. $12.50

FIVE CENTS.

3rd Grade
Math in Action

High Score

In a video game, gold coins are worth 1,000 points, silver coins are worth 100 points, red gems are worth 10 points, and blue gems are worth 1 point. WRITE the score for each player.

◯ = 1,000 points   ● = 100 points   ⬡ = 10 points   ⬡ = 1 point

Player 1	
◯ ◯	
● ● ● ●	
⬡	
⬡ ⬡ ⬡ ⬡ ⬡ ⬡ ⬡ ⬡	
Total Score	

Player 2	
◯ ◯ ◯ ◯ ◯	
● ● ●	
⬡ ⬡ ⬡ ⬡ ⬡	
⬡ ⬡ ⬡ ⬡ ⬡ ⬡	
Total Score	

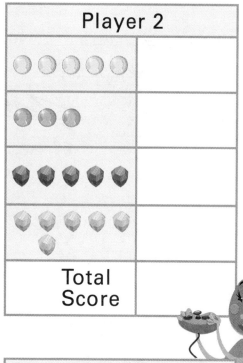

Player 3	
◯ ◯ ◯ ◯ ◯ ◯ ◯ ◯	
●	
⬡ ⬡	
⬡ ⬡ ⬡ ⬡	
Total Score	

Player 4	
◯ ◯ ◯ ◯	
● ● ● ● ● ● ●	
⬡ ⬡ ⬡ ⬡ ⬡	
⬡ ⬡	
Total Score	

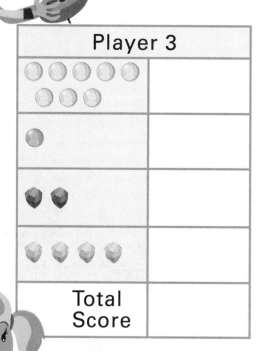

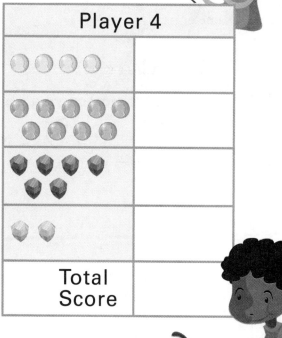

Check This Out

To write a check, the amount of the check must be written as both a number and number words. WRITE the number missing from each check.

1.

ADA BYRON   545

Date _Sept 1, 2010_

Pay to the
Order of _Mathton University_ $ **6,439**

Six thousand, four hundred thirty-nine _____ Dollars

Memo _____

A560000056A1020944332205C 545

2.

PAUL PYTHAGOREAS   322

Date _Aug 25, 2010_

Pay to the
Order of _Superbuy Appliances_ $ [   ]

Two thousand, five hundred six _____ Dollars

Memo _____

A320000032A10305646745C 322

3.

Dina Diameter   1062

Date _June 13, 2010_

Pay to the
Order of _Swanson's Swimming Pools_ $ [   ]

Four thousand, eight hundred fifty-two _____ **Dollars**

Memo _____

A650000065A202054361850C 1062

4.

Lloyd Wright   299

Date _JULY 5, 2010_

Pay to the
Order of _CONNIE'S CONSTRUCTION_ $ [   ]

ONE THOUSAND, NINE HUNDRED SEVENTEEN _____ Dollars

Memo _____

A120000012A50502652537C 299

Interesting Inventions

These dates show when these familiar things were invented. WRITE the numbers 1 through 10 so that 1 is the earliest invention and 10 is the most recent invention.

1. Light bulb   1835 _____

2. Roller coaster   1784 _____

3. E-mail   1971 _____

4. Telephone   1876 _____

5. MP3 player   1999 _____

6. Kaleidoscope   1816 _____

7. Piano   1700 _____

8. Zipper   1851 _____

9. Cell phone   1973 _____

10. Telescope   1609 _____

Piggy Bank

Each row shows money in and out of the piggy bank. CIRCLE the larger amount.

$4,329

$7,533

$3,580

$8,345

$4,932

High Score

The high scores on the left are sorted by name. WRITE a new high score list starting with the highest score and ending with the lowest score.

HIGH SCORES	
AVA	9,187
CAM	8,745
ELI	8,239
IAN	8,927
JOE	9,021
MAC	9,358
VAL	9,399
ZOE	7,864

HIGH SCORES		
1.		
2.		
3.		
4.		
5.		
6.		
7.		
8.		

City Stats

Each city is shown with the distance in kilometers to three other cities. CIRCLE the city that is closest.

1. London to

Hong Kong	9,646
Rome	1,434
Beijing	8,160

2. New York to

San Francisco	4,140
Paris	5,851
Caracas	3,419

3. Montreal to

Honolulu	7,915
Cairo	8,733
Rio de Janeiro	8,175

4. Tokyo to

Melbourne	8,159
Moscow	7,502
Stockholm	8,193

5. Singapore to

New Delhi	4,142
Cape Town	9,671
Beijing	4,465

6. Paris to

Montreal	5,522
Cairo	3,215
San Francisco	8,975

Price Fixer

Rounding makes numbers easier to work with. ROUND each price to the nearest hundred.

HINT: Numbers that end in 1 through 49 get rounded down to the nearest hundred, and numbers that end in 50 through 99 get rounded up to the nearest hundred.

$655

1

$976

2

$142

3

$438

4

$98

5

$368

6

$175

7

$250

8

Massive Mountains

ROUND the height of each mountain to the nearest thousand meters.

HINT: Numbers that end in 1 through 499 get rounded down to the nearest thousand, and numbers that end in 500 through 999 get rounded up to the nearest thousand.

1. Mount Everest   8,850 meters   _____ meters

2. The Matterhorn   4,478 meters   _____ meters

3. Mount Kilimanjaro   5,895 meters   _____ meters

4. Mount Ranier   4,392 meters   _____ meters

5. Makalu   8,485 meters   _____ meters

6. K12   7,428 meters   _____ meters

7. Mount Fuji   3,776 meters   _____ meters

8. Equinox Mountain   1,175 meters   _____ meters

9. Mount McKinley   6,194 meters   _____ meters

10. Mount Cook   3,754 meters   _____ meters

11. Mont Blanc   4,810 meters   _____ meters

12. Kula Kangri   7,538 meters   _____ meters

Going Green

If people drank water from the tap instead of from plastic bottles, those plastic bottles wouldn't end up in the landfill. The picture shows all of the plastic bottles thrown away from an office building in one day. ESTIMATE the number of bottles. Then COUNT to check your estimate.

Estimate: _____

Check: _____

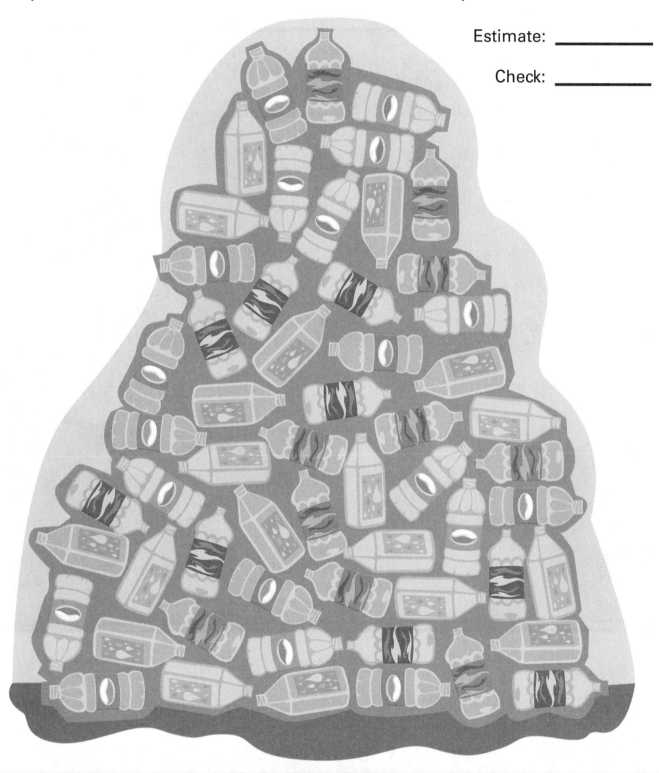

Bug Problem

Annie has a bug problem at her house so she called the exterminator, but the exterminator needs to know how many bugs there are. ESTIMATE the number of bugs. Then COUNT to check your estimate.

Estimate: _____   Check: _____

Flea Finds

The Fairway Flea Market is a great place for discovering treasures to add to all sorts of different collections. WRITE the total number of items in each person's collection after shopping at the flea market.

Ricky collects baseball cards. He has 72 baseball cards in his collection, and he bought 19 at the flea market.

1. How many baseball cards does Ricky have now? _____

Simon collects rare stamps and has 55 in his collection. He bought 22 at the flea market.

2. How many stamps does Simon have now? _____

Brittany has a collection of 58 comic books. She found a great deal at the flea market and bought 24 more.

3. How many comic books does Brittany have now? _____

Peter is just starting a collection of action figures. He has 17 in his collection, and he bought 16 more at the flea market.

4. How many action figures does Peter have now? _____

Sheila collects old buttons. She has 67 in her collection, and she bought a bag full of 35 buttons.

5. How many buttons does Sheila have now? _____

Adding & Subtracting 2-Digit Numbers

Piggy Bank

Each piggy bank shows how much money a kid has saved. If each kid takes $35 out of the bank to spend on a new video game, WRITE the new amount in each piggy bank.

$68

$ __33__
1

$45

$ _____
2

$39

$ _____
3

$50

$ _____
4

$92

$ _____
5

$74

$ _____
6

Calorie Counter

WRITE the total number of calories in each of these lunches. Then CIRCLE the lunch with the lowest number of calories.

Slice of pizza	328
Soda	212

Total calories: _____

1

Salad	299
Yogurt	124

Total calories: _____

2

Cheeseburger	326
French fries	287

Total calories: _____

3

Noodle soup	146
Turkey club sandwich	275

Total calories: _____

4

Save the Day

Wendy the Weekender always saves the day, as long as that day is a Saturday or Sunday. WRITE the total number of people she saved each weekend.

1. One Saturday Wendy saved 312 people, and that Sunday she saved 127 people. _____ people

2. One Saturday Wendy saved 254 people, and that Sunday she saved 416 people. _____ people

3. One Saturday Wendy saved 513 people, and that Sunday she saved 338 people. _____ people

4. One Saturday Wendy saved 699 people, and that Sunday she saved 262 people. _____ people

5. One Saturday Wendy saved 283 people, and that Sunday she saved 424 people. _____ people

6. One Saturday Wendy saved 494 people, and that Sunday she saved 320 people. _____ people

7. One Saturday Wendy saved 272 people, and that Sunday she saved 188 people. _____ people

8. One Saturday Wendy saved 695 people, and that Sunday she saved 217 people. _____ people

Driving Distances

WRITE the number of miles left on each person's drive.

Juan is driving 573 miles from Milwaukee to Kansas City.
He has driven 246 miles so far.

1. How many more miles does he have to drive? _____

Tallulah is driving 716 miles from Nashville to Baltimore.
She has driven 480 miles so far.

2. How many more miles does she have to drive? _____

Patrick is driving 642 miles from Pittsburg to Charleston.
He has driven 175 miles so far.

3. How many more miles does he have to drive? _____

Amy is driving 797 miles from New York to Chicago.
She has driven 638 miles so far.

4. How many more miles does she have to drive? _____

Ethan is driving 833 miles from Boise to Denver.
He has driven 527 miles so far.

5. How many more miles does he have to drive? _____

Maya is driving 750 miles from San Francisco to Phoenix.
She has driven 139 miles so far.

6. How many more miles does she have to drive? _____

Chicago   184
Milwaukee 279

That Does Not Compute!

The Great Roboto is on the fritz and is spitting out some math problems with wrong answers. CIRCLE the incorrect differences.

$$\begin{array}{r} 265 \\ -198 \\ \hline \boxed{167} \end{array}$$

$$\begin{array}{r} 930 \\ -327 \\ \hline 603 \end{array}$$

$$\begin{array}{r} 529 \\ -182 \\ \hline 347 \end{array}$$

$$\begin{array}{r} 488 \\ -293 \\ \hline 165 \end{array}$$

$$\begin{array}{r} 855 \\ -564 \\ \hline 291 \end{array}$$

$$\begin{array}{r} 434 \\ -190 \\ \hline 255 \end{array}$$

$$\begin{array}{r} 600 \\ -426 \\ \hline 274 \end{array}$$

$$\begin{array}{r} 810 \\ -282 \\ \hline 528 \end{array}$$

$$\begin{array}{r} 796 \\ -698 \\ \hline 98 \end{array}$$

$$\begin{array}{r} 608 \\ -362 \\ \hline 346 \end{array}$$

$$\begin{array}{r} 416 \\ -147 \\ \hline 269 \end{array}$$

$$\begin{array}{r} 947 \\ -473 \\ \hline 454 \end{array}$$

Ask the Judges

The winner of the dance competition is the dancer with the highest score out of 150 possible points. ADD each dancer's scores. Then CIRCLE the winning dancer.

46	50	36	48	39	47
42	49	44	48	46	38
38	43	41	48	40	45
1	2	3	4	5	6

Settle the Score

Four friends are playing a game, earning points for each turn. WRITE the total number of points for each person, and CIRCLE the person with the highest number of points.

SCORE			
Amanda	Masa	Jimmy	Rosa
45	22	14	45
23	54	48	19
37	45	36	56
30	29	33	27

High Score

These four kids are all trying to get the high score. ADD their scores, and CIRCLE the person with the highest score.

Player 1	
	512
	128
	97
Total Score	

Player 2	
	246
	352
	188
Total Score	

Player 3	
	267
	204
	219
Total Score	

Player 4	
	198
	344
	206
Total Score	

Sweet Sale

The members of the Bentonville School band are raising money for a trip to Germany, and they're holding bake sales in four different parts of town. WRITE the number of cakes, brownies, and cookies sold at each of the bake sales. Then WRITE the total number of treats sold at all of the bake sales.

1. At the first bake sale, the kids sold 144 cookies, 125 cupcakes, and 189 brownies.

   _____ treats

2. Across town the kids sold 113 cupcakes, 126 cookies, and 97 brownies.

   _____ treats

3. At the bake sale near the school the kids sold 157 cookies, 128 brownies, and 76 cupcakes.

   _____ treats

4. At the last bake sale they sold 177 brownies, 38 cupcakes, and 161 cookies.

   _____ treats

   Total: _____ treats

Book Bounty

Six small towns are starting new libraries and need more books. Fortunately a large book publisher has agreed to give each new library 1,275 books. WRITE the number of books each library will have once the new books arrive.

1. Park Ridge Library
$$6{,}458 \text{ books}$$
$$+1{,}275$$

2. Crystal Lake Library
$$4{,}913 \text{ books}$$
$$+1{,}275$$

3. Newburgh Library
$$8{,}072 \text{ books}$$
$$+1{,}275$$

4. Olive Falls Library
$$5{,}534 \text{ books}$$
$$+1{,}275$$

5. Salish Library
$$7{,}926 \text{ books}$$
$$+1{,}275$$

6. Washington Library
$$8{,}435 \text{ books}$$
$$+1{,}275$$

Adding & Subtracting 4-Digit Numbers

That Does Not Compute!

The Great Roboto is on the fritz and is spitting out some math problems with wrong answers. CIRCLE the incorrect sums.

```
  3,352
+ 1,014
-------
  4,366
```

```
  8,121
+   592
-------
  9,713
```

```
  1,128
+   806
-------
  1,934
```

```
  4,370
+ 2,726
-------
  6,196
```

```
  5,187
+   223
-------
  5,300
```

```
  7,707
+ 1,802
-------
  9,509
```

```
  2,193
+ 2,134
-------
  4,227
```

```
  5,061
+   955
-------
  5,016
```

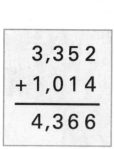

```
  3,166
+ 1,712
-------
  4,878
```

```
  4,358
+   992
-------
  4,250
```

```
  7,247
+   747
-------
  7,994
```

```
  2,922
+ 1,180
-------
  4,102
```

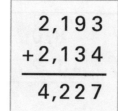

Best Price

Marty is shopping for the best price on a used car. Each car dealer has a similar car for a different price, and each is offering cash back on the purchase. CIRCLE the car with the best price after the cash back is subtracted.

$750 Cash Back — $5,325

CASH BACK!!! $275 — $4,950

$500 CASH BACK! — $5,095

CASH BACK $1,099 — $5,780

Mountain Marathon

The mountain marathon is an incredibly difficult race, heading 26 miles up the side of a mountain. It's so difficult that it takes up to 10 hours to complete, and most people don't make it to the finish line. This year, 9,348 people are running in the race. WRITE the number of people left in the race each hour.

1. At the two-hour mark, 527 people have dropped out of the race. _____

2. By the four-hour mark, 1,042 more people have dropped out of the race. _____

3. By the six-hour mark, 1,395 more people have dropped out of the race. _____

4. By the eight-hour mark, 2,178 more people have dropped out of the race. _____

5. For the rest of the race, only 384 people drop out. How many people finish this difficult mountain marathon? _____

That Does Not Compute!

The Great Roboto is on the fritz and is spitting out some math problems with wrong estimated answers. ESTIMATE each sum or difference by rounding to the nearest hundred. CIRCLE the incorrect estimates.

HINT: Numbers that end in 1 through 49 get rounded down to the nearest hundred, and numbers that end in 50 through 99 get rounded up to the nearest hundred.

768 + 219 = 900

910 − 478 = 300

568 + 123 = 700

456 + 438 = 900

881 − 579 = 200

642 − 335 = 300

1,245 + 1,567 = 2,800

3,410 − 2,213 = 1,600

4,479 + 3,099 = 6,500

8,531 − 7,466 = 2,000

5,068 + 1,927 = 6,600

7,714 − 3,425 = 4,300

Tennis Turnout

The chart shows the number of tickets sold for each tennis match. ESTIMATE the answers to the questions by rounding to the nearest thousand.

HINT: Numbers that end in 1 through 499 get rounded down to the nearest thousand, and numbers that end in 500 through 999 get rounded up to the nearest thousand.

Tennis Tournament Audience Turnout		
Match	Players	Tickets Sold
1	Federson vs. McEllis	2,108
2	Wilson vs. Prince	1,926
3	Rottick vs. Magnasy	3,237
4	Everest vs. Woudan	3,058
5	Federson vs. Magnasy	4,769
6	Wilson vs. Everest	4,885
7	Magnasy vs. Everest	8,231

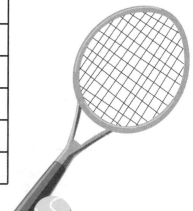

1. Approximately how many tickets were sold for Match 1 and Match 2 combined? _____

2. About how many more tickets were sold for Match 5 than Match 1? _____

3. About how many more tickets were sold for Match 7 than Match 5? _____

4. What was the approximate number of tickets sold for Matches 5, 6, and 7 combined? _____

5. What was the approximate number of tickets sold for all of the matches that Federson played? _____

6. What was the approximate number of tickets sold for all of the matches that Everest played? _____

Kate's Kitchen

Today in Kate's Kitchen, Kate is making easy school snacks. Each reusable container holds eight pieces of dried mango. WRITE the number of containers Kate will use to package all of the fruit.

_____ containers

Save the Day

Armie the Armazing has spotted 36 people trapped on the roof of a building, with giant spiders fast approaching. He can carry a total of 6 people, 3 under each of his amazingly long arms. WRITE the number of trips Armie must make to the building to rescue all of the people.

_____ trips

Once Upon a Time

A wolf blew down two pig houses, one made of straw and one made of sticks. The pigs fled to the brick house of the third pig, and they took all of their things with them. The little brick house is crowded. Each pig has the same number of things. WRITE the total number of each item now that the three little pigs are living together.

1. Each pig has six pans.   _____ total pans

2. Each pig has one stereo.   _____ total stereos

3. Each pig has four mittens.   _____ total mittens

4. Each pig has three paintings.   _____ total paintings

5. Each pig has five suitcases.   _____ total suitcases

6. Each pig has eight hats.   _____ total hats

7. Each pig has two lamps.   _____ total lamps

8. Each pig has seven pillows.   _____ total pillows

Kit Car

A kit to make your own model car comes with one car body, four wheels, five jars of paint, two paintbrushes, and eight stickers. WRITE the total number of pieces there are in different numbers of kits.

1. In 5 kits:

　　_____ car bodies

　　_____ wheels

　　_____ jars of paint

　　_____ paintbrushes

　　_____ stickers

2. In 10 kits:

　　_____ car bodies

　　_____ wheels

　　_____ jars of paint

　　_____ paintbrushes

　　_____ stickers

3. In 3 kits:

　　_____ car bodies

　　_____ wheels

　　_____ jars of paint

　　_____ paintbrushes

　　_____ stickers

4. In 7 kits:

　　_____ car bodies

　　_____ wheels

　　_____ jars of paint

　　_____ paintbrushes

　　_____ stickers

Skateboard Grinding

Sam at Sam's Skate-O-Rama makes custom skateboards. He makes nine skateboards a day.
WRITE the number of skateboards Sam has made after each of the combined number of days.

1. 1 day _____   2. 2 days _____

3. 3 days _____   4. 4 days _____

5. 5 days _____   6. 6 days _____

7. 7 days _____   8. 8 days _____

That Does Not Compute!

The Great Roboto is on the fritz and is spitting out some math problems with wrong answers.
CIRCLE the incorrect products.

$10 \times 3 = 30$

$0 \times 5 = 5$

$7 \times 6 = 43$

$8 \times 4 = 34$

$4 \times 10 = 44$

$9 \times 5 = 40$

$3 \times 1 = 3$

$10 \times 10 = 100$

$1 \times 1 = 2$

$2 \times 8 = 16$

$7 \times 8 = 56$

$3 \times 4 = 12$

$9 \times 9 = 81$

$2 \times 0 = 0$

$4 \times 5 = 20$

Super Soupy

The Super Soupy Soup Company just had a special contest. People who found a winning soup label won free soup. Six lucky winners found the labels for the grand prize, 54 cans of soup. WRITE the number of cans each winner receives if the winners share the soup equally.

_____ cans of soup

Once Upon a Time

Snow White has been picking mushrooms in the forest for the seven dwarves. She picked 49 mushrooms. WRITE the number of mushrooms each dwarf will get if the dwarves share the mushrooms equally.

_____ mushrooms

Party Time

Olivia is having six of her best friends over for a party, and she is going to give everyone a goodie bag. She wants to divide the goodies equally so each friend gets the same number of items. WRITE the number of each item that should go in each goodie bag.

1. 24 pieces of candy _____

2. 54 stickers _____

3. 6 pairs of sunglasses _____

4. 48 markers _____

5. 12 bouncy balls _____

6. 36 plastic animals _____

Dividing

Apple Picking

A class went on a field trip to an apple orchard. The kids were divided into groups of four and were told that they could evenly divide the apples among kids in the group when they were done. WRITE the number of apples each kid will get.

1. Group 1 picked 24 apples. Each kid in Group 1 will get _____ apples.

2. Group 2 picked 32 apples. Each kid in Group 2 will get _____ apples.

3. Group 3 picked 40 apples. Each kid in Group 3 will get _____ apples.

4. Group 4 picked 28 apples. Each kid in Group 4 will get _____ apples.

5. Group 5 picked 36 apples. Each kid in Group 5 will get _____ apples.

6. Group 6 picked 20 apples. Each kid in Group 6 will get _____ apples.

Make the Trade

READ the paragraph, and WRITE the answers.

Sid has a collection of 20 action figures that he doesn't play with anymore, so he's thinking about trading the action figures for some other toys. He could trade 5 action figures for one model car. He could trade 10 action figures for one building set. He could trade 4 action figures for one board game. He could trade 20 action figures for one video game. Sid only wants to trade for one kind of toy. How many of each toy would be needed to trade for all 20 of Sid's action figures?

1. _____ model cars

2. _____ building sets

3. _____ board games

4. _____ video games

On the Farm

Milo feeds all of the animals on the farm. WRITE the number of food items each animal gets.

1. Milo has 42 ears of corn to feed the 7 goats. Each goat gets _____ ears of corn.

2. Milo has 63 bundles of hay to feed the 9 horses. Each horse gets _____ bundles of hay.

3. Milo has 30 carrots to feed the 10 rabbits. Each rabbit gets _____ carrots.

4. Milo has 32 cups of grain to feed the 8 sheep. Each sheep gets _____ cups of grain.

5. Milo has 30 bundles of hay to feed the 6 cows. Each cow gets _____ bundles of hay.

6. Milo has 56 ears of corn to feed the 8 pigs. Each pig gets _____ ears of corn.

Fraction Magic

Merwin the Magician can saw his lovely assistant, Rita, in half. But he can also saw her into other fractions. WRITE the fraction of the box Rita's head will be in after Merwin works his magic.

$$\frac{1}{2}$$

1

2

3

4

Parts of a Whole

Kate's Kitchen

Today in Kate's Kitchen, Kate is making delicious parfait desserts. The desserts are made, but she wants to share the recipes. WRITE the missing fractions on each recipe card.

1. Chocolate-Strawberry Parfait

Fill glass with

_____ chocolate ice cream

_____ strawberries

_____ whipped cream

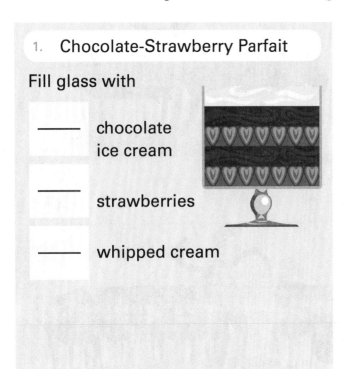

2. Berry-Burst Parfait

Fill glass with

_____ blueberries

_____ strawberries

_____ strawberry ice cream

_____ whipped cream

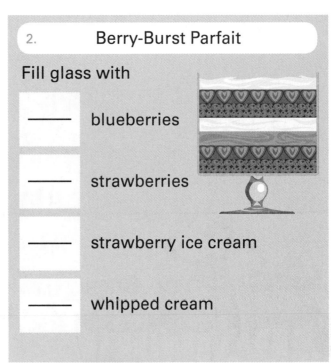

3. Kitchen Sink Parfait

Fill glass with

_____ blueberries

_____ strawberries

_____ bananas

_____ chocolate ice cream

_____ strawberry ice cream

Missing Pieces

WRITE the fraction of each puzzle that is missing.

_____

1

_____

2

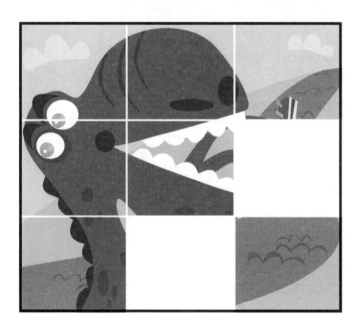

_____

3

_____

4

Subway Seats

One subway bench can seat six people. WRITE the fraction of seats taken on the subway bench after each stop.

1. At the first stop on the train, two people sit down on the bench. ⎯⎯

2. At the next station, one person gets off and three people sit down on the bench. ⎯⎯

3. One person gets off at the next station. ⎯⎯

4. At the next station, three people get on and sit down on the bench. ⎯⎯

5. Six people get off at the next station, and one person gets in and sits down on the bench. ⎯⎯

6. Four people sit down on the bench at the next station. ⎯⎯

Alien Invasion

Five aliens have landed, and it's your job to record information about them. WRITE the fraction that matches each description of the aliens.

1. Fraction of aliens with four legs ——

2. Fraction of aliens wearing purple ——

3. Fraction of aliens with one antenna ——

4. Fraction of aliens that are red ——

5. Fraction of aliens with more than two legs ——

6. Fraction of aliens with fewer than four eyes ——

Going Green

WRITE the fraction of the trash that can be recycled into each bin.

metal	plastic	paper
—	—	—
1	2	3

Art Museum

A museum is logging information about its art collection. WRITE the fraction that matches each description of the paintings.

1. Portraits are pictures of people. What fraction of the paintings are portraits? ——

2. Paintings of objects like fruit or flowers are called still lifes. What fraction of the paintings are still lifes? ——

3. Paintings of outside places are called landscapes. What fraction of the paintings are landscapes? ——

4. Paintings that do not look like pictures of a person, thing, or place are called abstract. What fraction of the paintings are abstract? ——

Field Trip

GO to an outdoor place like a park and FIND eight people. WRITE information about each person in the chart. Then ANSWER the questions.

	Person 1	Person 2	Person 3	Person 4	Person 5	Person 6	Person 7	Person 8
Boy or girl?								
Hair color?								
Wearing jeans?								
Wearing a hat?								
Carrying a bag?								

1. What fraction of the people are boys? ——

2. What fraction of the people are girls? ——

3. What fraction of the people have brown hair? 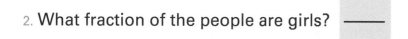 ——

4. What fraction of the people are wearing jeans?  ——

5. What fraction of the people are not wearing a hat?  ——

6. What fraction of the people have a bag? 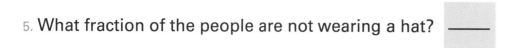 ——

Ferris Wheel

Look at the Ferris wheel, and WRITE the fraction that matches each description. CIRCLE the larger fraction in each pair.

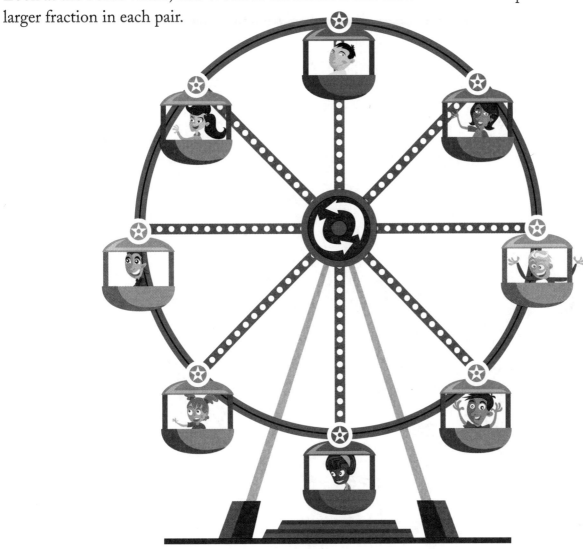

1. Fraction of riders who are girls ———

   Fraction of riders with black hair ———

2. Fraction of riders with blond hair ———

   Fraction of girls with red hair ———

3. Fraction of green cars ———

   Fraction of blue cars ———

4. Fraction of blue cars with boys ———

   Fraction of green cars with girls ———

That Does Not Compute!

The Great Roboto is on the fritz and is spitting out some wrong fractions. He was programmed to print pictures of fractions less than $\frac{2}{3}$. CIRCLE the pictures that are not less than $\frac{2}{3}$.

Kate's Kitchen

Today in Kate's Kitchen, Kate is making a chicken and vegetable stir-fry. DRAW lines to show where to cut each food.

Chicken and Vegetable Stir-Fry

Cut green onions into 3-inch pieces.
Cut carrot into 2-inch pieces.
Cut chicken into 1-inch strips.

Sauté in pan with sesame oil and soy sauce until the chicken is fully cooked and the vegetables are tender. Serve over rice.

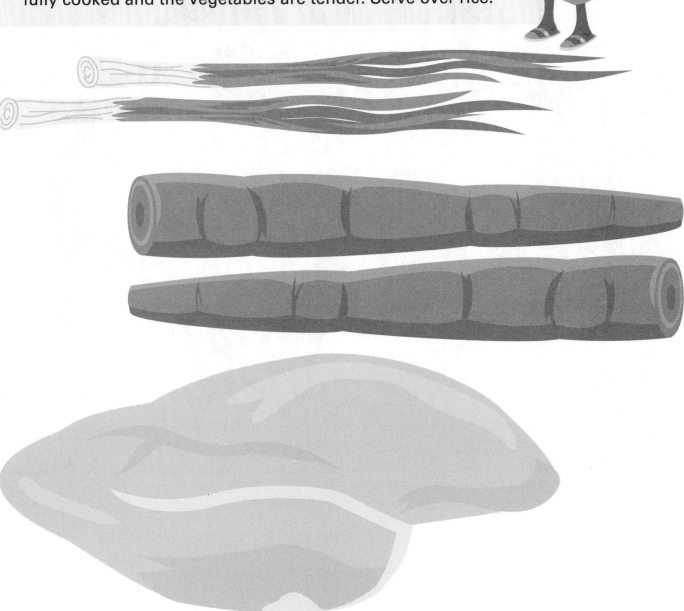

Once Upon a Time

"My, what big teeth you have," Little Red Riding Hood said to the wolf, who was posing as Red's grandmother. Red is not sure this is her grandmother. Help her know for sure by measuring the different features. WRITE each measurement in centimeters.

1. Fang: _____ centimeters

2. Eye: _____ centimeters

3. Claw: _____ centimeters

Missing Measurements

All of these items have been measured, but each is missing its unit of measure. WRITE *inches*, *feet*, or *yards* after each measurement.

HINT: Remember, 1 foot is equal to 12 inches, and 1 yard is equal to 3 feet.

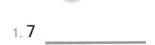

1. **7** _____

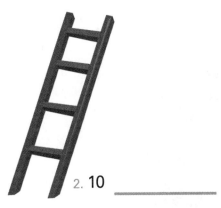

2. **10** _____

3. **33** _____

4. **15** _____

5. **6** _____

6. **12** _____

That Can't Be Right

CIRCLE the person who is most likely stretching the truth.

I caught a fish that was 1 foot long. It made a delicious dinner for a friend and me.

I caught a fish that was 6 inches long. I decided to throw it back because it was too small.

I caught a fish that was 1 yard long. It was bigger than my boat so I couldn't keep it.

I was so excited to catch my first fish. It was 14 inches long—bigger than all of the other fish that were caught today.

Shopping List

Each person is at a store that doesn't have milk in the size that matches the shopping list. CIRCLE the containers of equal volume that each person can buy.

2 cups = 1 pint

2 pints = 1 quart

4 quarts = 1 gallon

---

1 QUART OF MILK

1 GALLON OF MILK

---

3 PINTS OF MILK

2 QUARTS OF MILK

Missing Measurements

All of these items have been measured, but each is missing its unit of measure. WRITE *liters* or *milliliters* after each measurement.

HINT: Remember, 1 liter is equal to 1,000 milliliters.

1. 2 _____

2. 750 _____

3. 50 _____

4. 150 _____

5. 150 _____

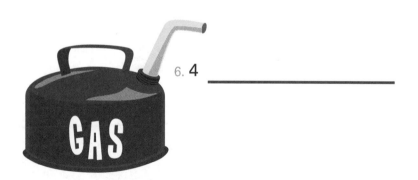

6. 4 _____

That Can't Be Right

CIRCLE the person who is most likely stretching the truth.

I was so thirsty the other day! I drank a quart of orange juice all by myself.

I do not like milk at all. I have a hard time even drinking the cup of milk that my dad puts in my lunch every day.

We went to the super bulk store last week, and we bought a jar of mayonnaise that could hold a whole gallon. You should see the size of this jar!

There is nothing I love more than milk on my cereal. Each morning I have a bowl of cereal, and I pour a gallon of milk on top.

Grocery Getter

Head into your kitchen and find 10 things that are measured in liquid volume. WRITE the name and volume of each thing you find. CIRCLE the grocery item that has the largest volume.

HINT: Look for measurements labeled either mL (milliliters) or fl oz (fluid ounces).

Grocery Item	Volume

Martha's Movers

Martha's Movers asks people to label each box with its contents and its weight. CIRCLE the boxes that most likely have the wrong measurement.

HINT: 1 pound = 16 ounces

Clothes
125
pounds

Dishes
36
ounces

Books
55
pounds

Pillows
4
pounds

Missing Measurements

All of these items have been measured, but each is missing its unit of measure. WRITE *ounces* or *pounds* after each measurement.

1. **10** _____

2. **12** _____

3. **320** _____

4. **23** _____

5. **36** _____

6. **4** _____

Amusement Adventures

One game people like to play at the amusement park is Guess My Weight, where Lester the Guesser guesses a person's weight. If he's wrong, the person gets a prize. CIRCLE the people who should get a prize.

HINT: The average weight for a 35-year-old man is around 80 kilograms.

KG

56 kilograms

18 kilograms

104 kilograms

99 kilograms

That Can't Be Right

CIRCLE the person who is most likely stretching the truth.

We took my puppy to the vet yesterday, and he weighed in at 5 kilograms already. Can you believe how big he's getting?

My mom sent me to the grocery store with a huge list. I had to carry home 40 kilograms of groceries all by myself!

I was so hungry when I went to the movies that I ate 250 grams of popcorn all by myself.

I found this gigantic caterpillar in my backyard yesterday. That thing must have weighed at least 100 grams!

Traveler's Forecast

The Park family lives in New York City, and they want to leave for a trip to someplace warmer.
WRITE the names of the cities they could visit where it will likely be warmer.

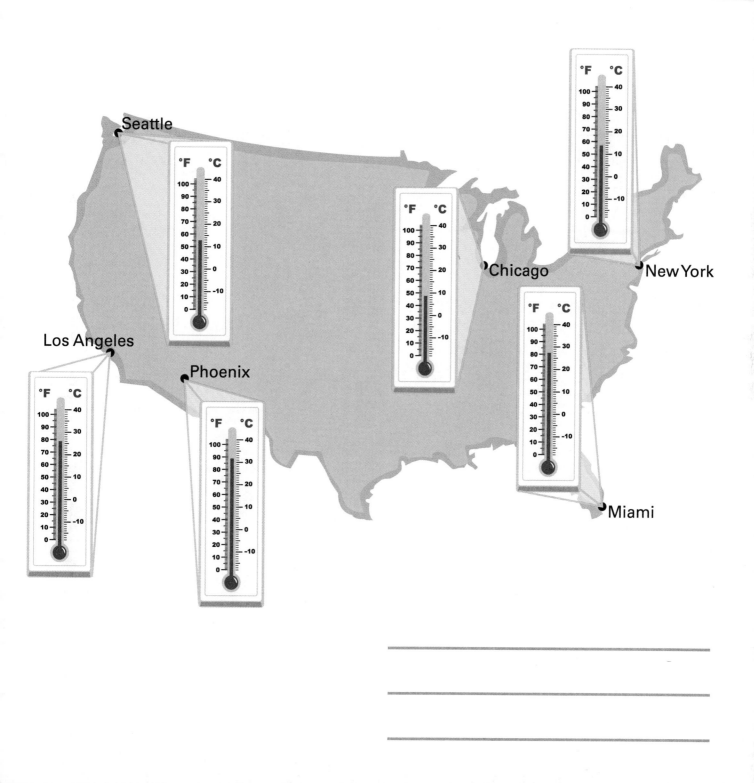

_____

_____

_____

Weather or Not

High temperatures tend to be similar from day to day in each city. CIRCLE the thermometer for each city if it shows a likely high temperature for Saturday.

High Temperatures	Mon	Tues	Wed	Thur	Fri	Sat
Dallas	87°F	95°F	91°F	82°F	85°F	
Denver	62°F	61°F	68°F	60°F	65°F	
Philadelphia	71°F	75°F	75°F	72°F	80°F	
Toronto	14°C	14°C	16°C	15°C	13°C	

Quality Quilts

Quilts are often made from repeated patterns of squares, where each square is made from a set of shapes. DRAW and COLOR a quilt square to match the ones shown.

HINT: You can make straight lines by tracing along the side of a ruler.

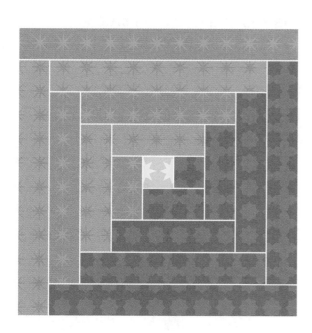
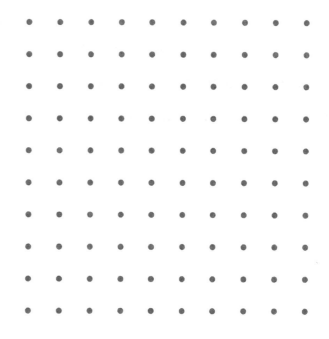

Custom Cakes

At Carla's Custom Cakes, a cake can be made in any shape with any kind of frosted decoration. READ each order. Then WRITE each person's name under the right cake.

HINT: A vertex is where two lines meet. A side is the line between two vertices.

Jane ordered a cake with four sides. The toppings each have three vertices.

Brent ordered a cake with five sides. The toppings each have four vertices.

Betsy ordered a cake with six sides. The toppings each have four vertices.

Walter ordered a cake with four sides. The toppings each have five vertices.

1

2

3

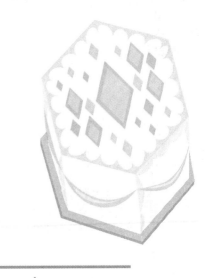

4

Where I Live

This is a drawing of my bedroom, my house, and my block, and I want to know the perimeter of each one. WRITE the perimeters.

HINT: To find the perimeter of something, add the length of each side.

88 yards

200 yards

MY BLOCK

MY ROOM
12 feet × 10 feet

MY HOUSE
22 feet × 25 feet

1. Bedroom perimeter: _____ feet

2. House perimeter: _____ feet

3. Block perimeter: _____ yards

Carpet Crazy

The Carpenter family is crazy about carpet, and they're having it installed in every room of their new home. WRITE the area of each room on their carpet order

HINT: To find the area of a room, multiply the length by the width. The answer will be in square feet (sq ft).

Cary's Carpet Emporium Order Form			
Carpet	**Room**	**Room Dimensions**	**Area**
Lime-green Berber	Living room	10 ft × 10 ft	1. _____ sq ft
Blue plush	Master bedroom	8 ft × 10 ft	2. _____ sq ft
Yellow short pile	Small bedroom	9 ft × 8 ft	3. _____ sq ft
Purple Saxony	Kitchen	7 ft × 10 ft	4. _____ sq ft
Pink shag	Dining room	9 ft × 9 ft	5. _____ sq ft
Striped loop pile	Bathroom	6 ft × 7 ft	6. _____ sq ft

Buildings of the World

CIRCLE the shape that each building most closely resembles.

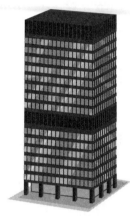

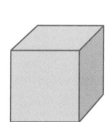

The Federal Center
Chicago

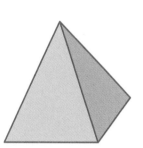

The Louvre Pyramid
Paris

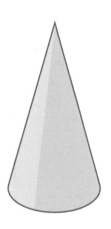

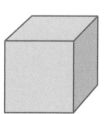

The Capitol Records building
Los Angeles

Shaded Shapes

You can use color to make drawn shapes look three dimensional. Using three different shades of the same color, SHADE each shape to look three dimensional

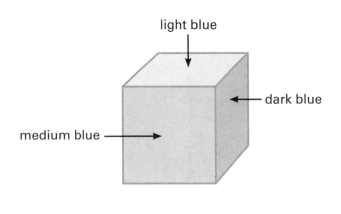

light blue

dark blue

medium blue

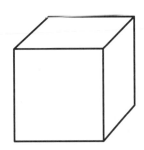

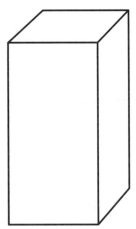

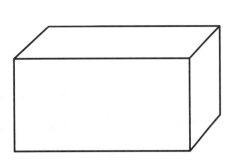

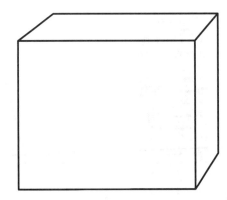

Shopper's Search

CIRCLE the package that each person is describing.

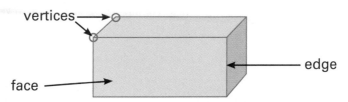

vertices
edge
face

1. Can you help me? I'm looking for a box that has all square faces and eight vertices.

2. My daughter wants the toy that comes in a box that has six faces, two of which are squares.

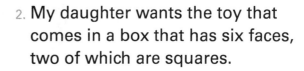

3. I like candy with triangular faces and eight edges.

Save the Day

Owlboy has finally caught the diabolical criminal Two Square Face. He is known for stealing only precious crystals that have at least two square faces. CIRCLE the crystals that came from Two Square Face's hideout.

Game Designer

You're a game designer making a level for the new Chaos Crusaders video game. The screen of this level is going to be perfectly symmetrical. DRAW and COLOR the rest of the screen.

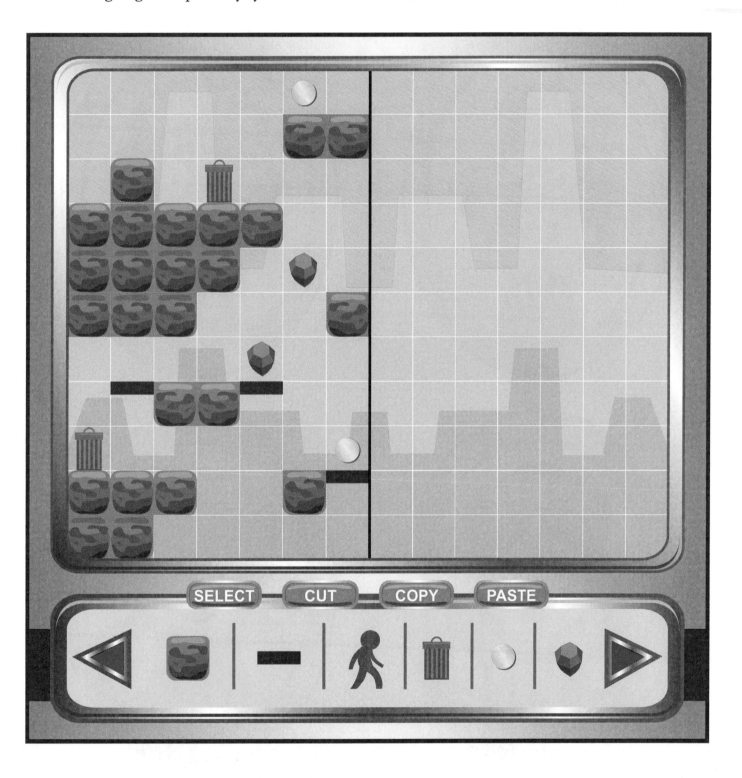

Once Upon a Time

Mirror, Mirror, on the fireplace, who has the most symmetrical face? CIRCLE the princess whose reflection is perfectly symmetrical.

Printer Problems

Peter is having problems with his printer. The picture on the left shows what the picture should look like, and the picture on the right shows what was printed. WRITE *flip*, *slide*, or *turn* for each picture.

1. _____

2. _____

3. _____

4. _____

Flip and Turn

COLOR each shape to show the first shape flipped and turned.

	Flip	Turn

Zoned Out

The world is divided into many different time zones. While it might be 2:00 in the afternoon where you live, it's 2:00 in the morning somewhere else. These clocks show the local time on the same day in different cities. WRITE the time difference between each pair of cities.

Tokyo
10:00 p.m.

Dubai
5:00 p.m.

London
1:00 p.m.

New York
8:00 a.m.

Denver
6:00 a.m.

Honolulu
3:00 a.m.

1. New York and London _____ hours

2. Dubai and Tokyo _____ hours

3. Honolulu and Denver _____ hours

4. Denver and Dubai _____ hours

5. New York and Tokyo _____ hours

6. Honolulu and London _____ hours

7. Denver and London _____ hours

8. New York and Dubai _____ hours

9. Honolulu and Tokyo _____ hours

10. London and Tokyo _____ hours

Adding & Subtracting Time

Great Strides

One of the best-known marathons is the Boston Marathon. The chart shows some of the winning times for men and women in the marathon's history. LOOK at the chart, and ANSWER the questions.

Year	Men's Open Winner	Women's Open Winner
2009	2 hours, 8 minutes, 42 seconds	2 hours, 32 minutes, 16 seconds
2000	2 hours, 9 minutes, 47 seconds	2 hours, 26 minutes, 11 seconds
1994	2 hours, 7 minutes, 15 seconds	2 hours, 21 minutes, 45 seconds
1973	2 hours, 16 minutes, 3 seconds	3 hours, 5 minutes, 59 seconds
1966	2 hours, 17 minutes, 11 seconds	3 hours, 21 minutes, 40 seconds

1. What is the difference in time between the winner of the Men's Open and Women's Open in 1966? _____ hour, _____ minutes, _____ seconds

2. What is the difference in time between the winner of the Men's Open and Women's Open in 2009? _____ minutes, _____ seconds

3. How much faster was the time of the winner of the Men's Open in 2000 than in 1973? _____ minutes, _____ seconds

4. How much faster was the time of the winner of the Women's Open in 2000 than in 1973? _____ minutes, _____ seconds

5. What is the difference in time between the fastest and slowest time shown in the chart? _____ hour, _____ minutes, _____ seconds

TV Time

Allison loves her favorite shows. WRITE how much time she spends watching each show in a week. Then WRITE the total time Allison spends watching TV in a week.

			Hours	Minutes
1.	*The Magic Morning Show*	1 hour and 30 minutes, 3 days a week		
2.	*Kid's Komedy Korner*	30 minutes, 5 days a week		
3.	*Life on a Boat*	1 hour, 2 days a week		
4.	*Paparazzi Parade*	45 minutes, 3 days a week		
5.	*Fashion Forward*	15 minutes, 5 days a week		
6.	*Real Nature*	30 minutes, 2 days a week		
		7. Total		

Toy Crafting

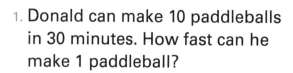

Donald has a job making toys, and he's very fast at his job. WRITE the time it takes him to make one of each toy.

1. Donald can make 10 paddleballs in 30 minutes. How fast can he make 1 paddleball?

_____ minutes

2. Donald can make five dolls in 45 minutes. How fast can he make one doll?

_____ minutes

3. Donald can make six cars in 42 minutes. How fast can he make one car?

_____ minutes

4. Donald can make eight robots in 1 hour and 20 minutes. How fast can he make one robot?

_____ minutes

5. Donald can make nine dollhouses in 1 hour and 12 minutes. How fast can he make one dollhouse?

_____ minutes

Vending Machine

LOOK at the prices on the vending machine, and ANSWER the questions.

1. How much would it cost to buy a bag of potato chips and a bag of dried apples? $ _____

2. How much would it cost to buy a bag of trail mix, a bag of pretzels, and a bag of corn chips? $ _____

3. What two things could you buy for exactly $1.85?

_____

4. What two things could you buy for exactly $2.55?

_____

5. If you put $1.00 in the machine and bought a bag of pretzels, how much change would you get? $ _____

6. If you put $5.00 in the machine and bought a granola bar, how much change would you get? $ _____

Change Chooser

Michael doesn't like to carry around a lot of coins or small bills. Whenever he can, he uses extra coins and bills so he receives no coins or one-dollar bills in change. CIRCLE the money he should use to get the least amount of change back in only five-dollar bills or larger. Then WRITE the amount of change he should get.

$13.62

1. Change $ _____

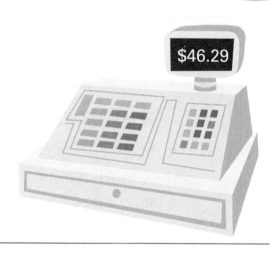

$46.29

2. Change $ _____

$72.98

3. Change $ _____

Cab Fare

A cab ride costs $2.50 just to get in the cab, and then $2.00 per mile. WRITE the total fare for each of the cab rides.

1. 8 miles $ 18.50

2. 2 miles $ _____

3. 5 miles $ _____

4. 1 miles $ _____

5. 9 miles $ _____

6. 7 miles $ _____

7. 10 miles $ _____

8. 4 miles $ _____

9. 6 miles $ _____

10. 3 miles $ _____

By the Pound

WRITE the cost of one pound of each food item.

1. Six pounds for $6.00

   $_____ per pound

2. Eight pounds for $16.00

   $_____ per pound

3. Four pounds for $36.00

   $_____ per pound

4. Three pounds for $30.00

   $_____ per pound

5. Two pounds for $15.00

   $_____ per pound

6. Three pounds for $3.75

   $_____ per pound

Get Going

In this graph, one picture is equal to one person. LOOK at the graph, and ANSWER the questions.

Ways Students Get to School

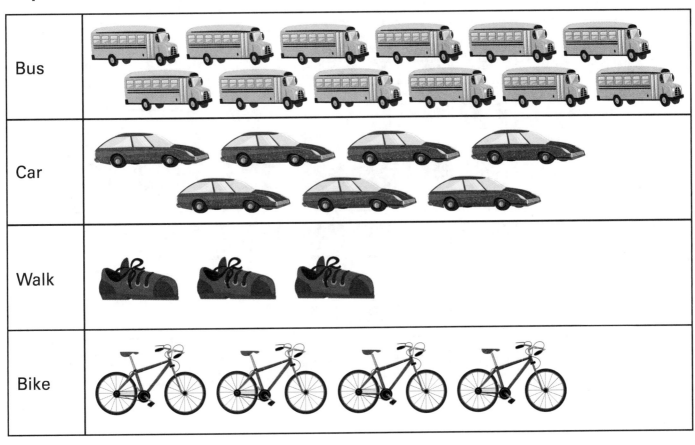

1. How many students walk to school? _____

2. How many students take the bus to school? _____

3. How many more students take a car than bike to school? _____

4. How many more students take the bus than walk to school? _____

5. How likely is it that the next student you ask takes the bus to school?

      impossible   unlikely   likely   certain

6. How likely is it that the next student you ask walks to school?

      impossible   unlikely   likely   certain

Picture Graphs

What Are You Watching?

This graph shows kids' favorite kinds of TV shows. Each TV picture is equal to five kids. LOOK at the graph, and ANSWER the questions.

Favorite Types of TV Shows

 = 5 kids

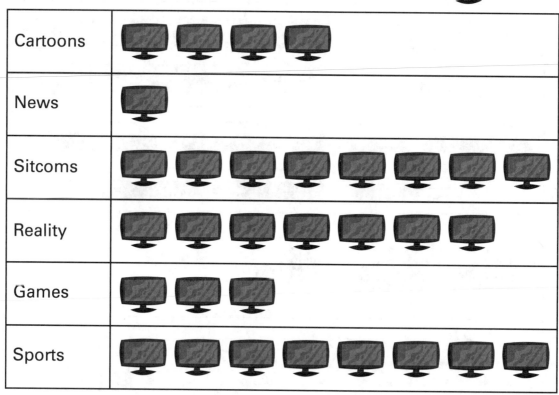

1. How many kids say reality shows are their favorite type of show? _____

2. What is the least popular type of show? _____

3. What two types of shows did an equal number of kids list as their favorite?

_____

4. How many kids say sitcoms, cartoons, or sports shows are their favorite type of show? _____

5. How many more kids like sitcoms than game shows? _____

6. How many kids are represented in this graph? _____

Sweet Sale

The local scout troop is selling candy bars to raise money to improve the neighborhood park. LOOK at the graph, and ANSWER the questions.

Candy Bars Sold

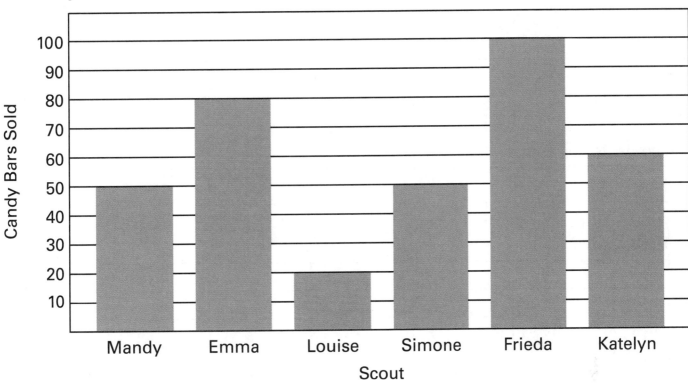

1. How many candy bars did Katelyn sell? _____

2. How many candy bars did Emma sell? _____

3. Which two scouts sold the same number of candy bars? _____

4. Who sold the most candy bars? _____

5. If Louise wanted to sell as many candy bars as Frieda, how many more would she have to sell? _____

6. What is the total number of candy bars sold by the scout troop? _____

Graph It

ASK 15 kids what job they would like to have when they're older. RECORD their answers with tally marks in the chart. Then DRAW the graph.

Doctor	
Teacher	
President	
Astronaut	
Video-game designer	
Other	

Dream Jobs

Number of People	Doctor	Teacher	President	Astronaut	Video-Game Designer	Other
15						
14						
13						
12						
11						
10						
9						
8						
7						
6						
5						
4						
3						
2						
1						

Dream Job

Favorite Color

Fifty people were asked their favorite color. LOOK at the results shown in the graph, and ANSWER the questions.

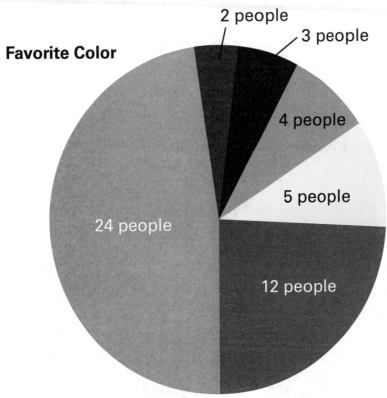

Favorite Color

2 people

3 people

4 people

5 people

24 people

12 people

1. What is the most popular favorite color? _____

2. What is the least popular favorite color? _____

3. How many more people prefer red to yellow? _____

4. How many more people prefer blue to green? _____

5. About what fraction of people have the favorite color blue?

$\frac{1}{4}$ $\frac{1}{3}$ $\frac{1}{2}$ $\frac{3}{4}$

6. About what fraction of people have the favorite color red?

$\frac{1}{4}$ $\frac{1}{3}$ $\frac{1}{2}$ $\frac{3}{4}$

Pick a Graph

READ the paragraph, and CIRCLE the graph that works best with the title "What Hannah Did on Monday."

Hannah wanted to graph how she spent her Monday. She spent eight hours sleeping and seven hours at school. She watched TV for two hours and was at karate class for two hours. Three hours were spent reading or doing homework and one hour eating. She spent one hour of the day doing other little things.

Which graph shows what Hannah did on Monday?

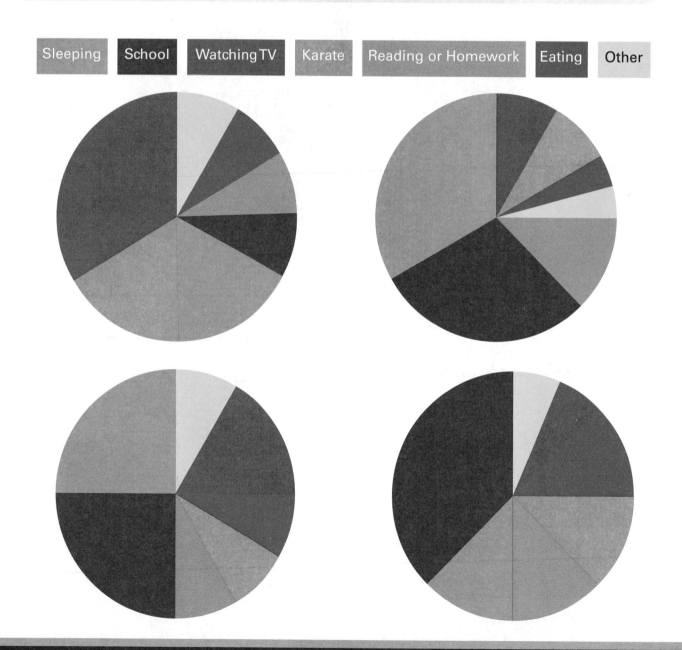

Home Run!

This line plot shows the number of home runs hit in a season by each player of the baseball team. Each X represents one player. LOOK at the line plot, and ANSWER the questions.

Home Runs

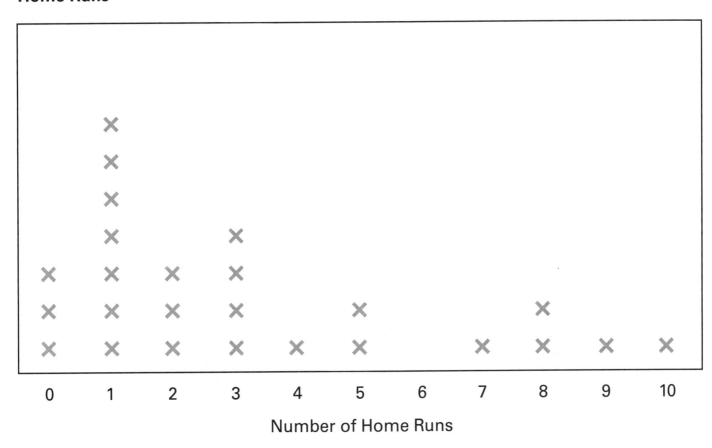

Number of Home Runs

1. How many players hit exactly five home runs this season? _____

2. How many players hit exactly six home runs? _____

3. How many players hit no home runs? _____

4. How many players hit seven or more home runs? _____

5. How many players hit five or fewer home runs? _____

6. How many players are on the team? _____

Planning Parties

Some friends are curious about what months will have the most birthday parties. Each X represents a person who has a birthday that month. LOOK at the line plot, and ANSWER the questions.

Birthday Months

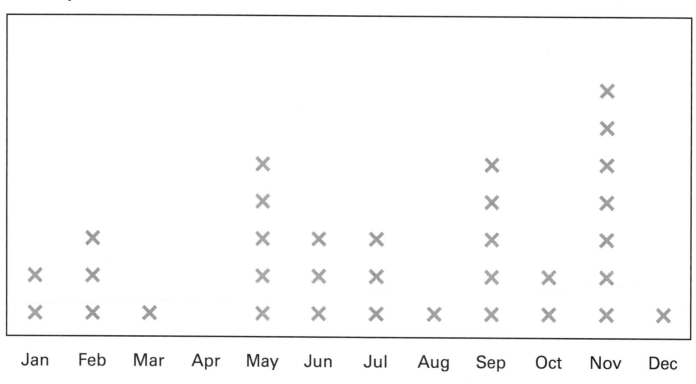

1. How many people have birthdays in June? _____

2. How many people have birthdays in September? _____

3. How many people have birthdays in January, February, and December combined?

_____

4. How many more people have a birthday in November than in March? _____

5. What three months have the most birthdays? _____

6. If all of the people have a party in the same month as their birthday, in what month will there be no birthday party? _____

Saving Up

Sam is saving to buy a $120 bicycle. He has been saving for six months and graphs his progress at the end of each month. LOOK at the graph, and ANSWER the questions.

Sam's Savings

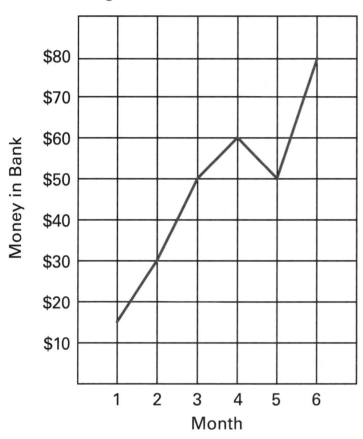

1. At the end of which month did Sam have about $15 saved? _____

2. How much money did Sam have saved at the end of month 2? _____

3. How much money did Sam have saved at the end of month 4? _____

4. How much money did Sam save in six months? _____

5. In what month did Sam spend some of the money he was saving? _____

6. How likely is it that Sam will have enough money for his bike in three more months?

   impossible   unlikely   likely   certain

Let's Grow

Alyssa is growing basil and lavender from seeds on her windowsill. She records the plant heights each week. LOOK at the graph, and ANSWER the questions.

Plant Growth

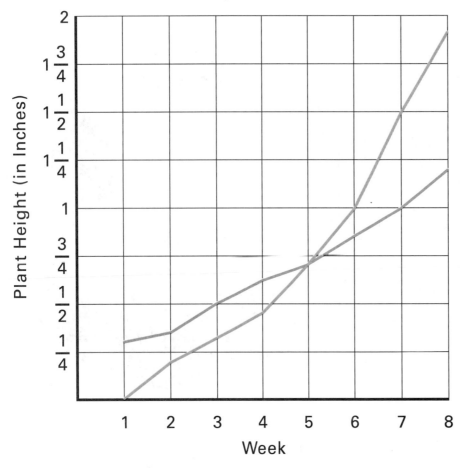

1. Which plant was taller at week 1? _____

2. Which plant was taller at week 7? _____

3. In which week was the lavender one inch tall? _____

4. In which week was the basil one inch tall? _____

5. In which week were the plants about the same height? _____

6. At the end of eight weeks, which plant was closer to being two inches tall? _____

Graph It

FILL IN the graph with data you collect from weather reports in your area. For every day of the week, RECORD both the high and low temperature. Use a red line to connect the high temperatures and a blue line to connect the low temperatures. Use your graph to ANSWER the questions.

My Weather Chart

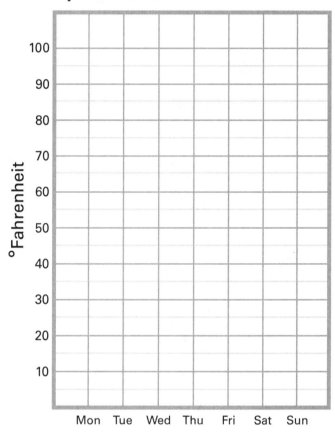

—— High temperatures
—— Low temperatures

1. What day was the warmest? _____

2. What was the high temperature on that day? _____

3. What day was the coldest? _____

4. What was the low temperature on that day? _____

CIRCLE the best answer.

5. Next week, it is **likely/unlikely** to reach a high temperature of 80°F.

6. Next week, it is **likely/unlikely** to reach a high temperature of 50°F.

7. Next week, it is **likely/unlikely** to reach a low temperature of 5°F.

Answers

Page 213
Player 1: 2,418
Player 2: 5,356
Player 3: 8,124
Player 4: 4,962

Page 214
1. 6,439
2. 2,506
3. 4,852
4. 1,917

Page 215
1. 5
2. 3
3. 8
4. 7
5. 10
6. 4
7. 2
8. 6
9. 9
10. 1

Page 216

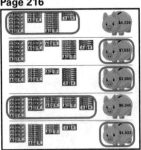

Page 217
1. VAL 9,399
2. MAC 9,358
3. AVA 9,187
4. JOE 9,021
5. IAN 8,927
6. CAM 8,745
7. ELI 8,239
8. ZOE 7,864

Page 218
1. Rome
2. Caracas
3. Honolulu
4. Moscow
5. New Delhi
6. Cairo

Page 219
1. $700
2. $1,000
3. $100
4. $400
5. $100
6. $400
7. $200
8. $300

Page 220
1. 9,000
2. 4,000
3. 6,000
4. 4,000
5. 8,000
6. 7,000
7. 4,000
8. 1,000
9. 6,000
10. 4,000
11. 5,000
12. 8,000

Page 221
Check: 57

Page 222
Check: 82

Page 223
1. 91
2. 77
3. 82
4. 33
5. 102

Page 224
1. 33
2. 10
3. 4
4. 15
5. 57
6. 39

Page 225
1. 540
2. 423
3. 613
4. 421

Page 226
1. 439
2. 670
3. 851
4. 961
5. 707
6. 814
7. 460
8. 912

Page 227
1. 327
2. 236
3. 467
4. 159
5. 306
6. 611

Page 228

Page 229
1. 126
2. 142
3. 121
4. 144
5. 125
6. 130

Page 230

Amanda	Masa	Jimmy	Rosa
45	22	14	45
23	54	48	19
37	45	36	56
30	29	33	27
135	150	131	147

Page 231
Player 1: 737
Player 2: 786
Player 3: 690
Player 4: 748

Page 232
1. 458
2. 336
3. 361
4. 376
Total: 1,531

Page 233
1. 7,733
2. 6,188
3. 9,347
4. 6,809
5. 9,201
6. 9,710

Page 234

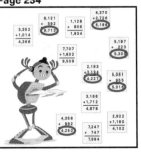

Page 235

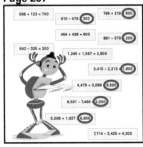

Page 236
1. 8,821
2. 7,779
3. 6,384
4. 4,206
5. 3,822

Page 237

Page 238
1. 4,000
2. 3,000
3. 3,000
4. 18,000
5. 7,000
6. 16,000

Page 239
4

Page 240
6

Page 241
1. 18
2. 3
3. 12
4. 9
5. 15
6. 24
7. 6
8. 21

Page 242
1. 5, 20, 25, 10, 40
2. 10, 40, 50, 20, 80
3. 3, 12, 15, 6, 24
4. 7, 28, 35, 14, 56

Page 243
1. 9
2. 18
3. 27
4. 36
5. 45
6. 54
7. 63
8. 72

Page 244

Page 245
9

Page 246
7

Page 247
1. 4
2. 9
3. 1
4. 8
5. 2
6. 6

Page 248
1. 6
2. 8
3. 10
4. 7
5. 9
6. 5

Page 249
1. 4
2. 2
3. 5
4. 1

Page 250
1. 6
2. 7
3. 3
4. 4
5. 5
6. 7

Page 251
1. $\frac{1}{3}$
2. $\frac{1}{6}$
3. $\frac{1}{4}$
4. $\frac{1}{7}$

Page 252
1. $\frac{2}{5}$, $\frac{2}{5}$, $\frac{1}{5}$
2. $\frac{2}{7}$, $\frac{2}{7}$, $\frac{1}{7}$, $\frac{2}{7}$
3. $\frac{2}{10}$, $\frac{1}{10}$, $\frac{3}{10}$, $\frac{3}{10}$, $\frac{1}{10}$

Page 253
1. $\frac{2}{8}$
2. $\frac{3}{10}$
3. $\frac{2}{9}$
4. $\frac{5}{12}$

Page 254
1. $\frac{2}{6}$
2. $\frac{4}{6}$
3. $\frac{3}{6}$
4. $\frac{6}{6}$
5. $\frac{1}{6}$
6. $\frac{5}{6}$

Page 255

1. $\frac{3}{5}$ 2. $\frac{2}{5}$

3. $\frac{3}{5}$ 4. $\frac{1}{5}$

5. $\frac{4}{5}$ 6. $\frac{3}{5}$

Page 256

1. $\frac{2}{9}$ 2. $\frac{4}{9}$ 3. $\frac{3}{9}$

Page 257

1. $\frac{3}{8}$ 2. $\frac{2}{8}$

3. $\frac{1}{8}$ 4. $\frac{2}{8}$

Page 258
Have someone check
your answers.

Page 259

1. $\frac{4}{8}$, $\boxed{\frac{5}{8}}$ 2. $\frac{1}{8}$, $\boxed{\frac{1}{4}}$

3. $\boxed{\frac{4}{8}}$, $\frac{2}{8}$ 4. $\boxed{\frac{2}{2}}$, $\frac{3}{4}$

Page 260

Page 261

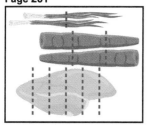

Page 262
1. 2 2. 3 3. 1

Page 263
1. inches 2. feet 3. inches
4. yards 5. feet 6. yards

Page 264

Page 265

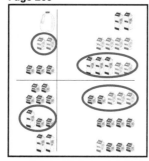

Page 266
1. liters
2. milliliters
3. milliliters
4. liters
5. milliliters
6. liters

Page 267

Page 268
Have someone check
your answers.

Page 269

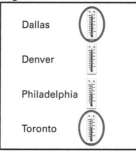

Page 270
1. pounds 2. ounces
3. pounds 4. pounds
5. ounces 6. ounces

Page 271

Page 272

Page 273
Miami, Phoenix, Los Angeles

Page 274

Dallas

Denver

Philadelphia

Toronto

Page 275
Have someone check
your answers.

Page 276
1. Jane   2. Walter
3. Brent   4. Betsy

Page 277
1. 44   2. 94   3. 576

Page 278
1. 100 2. 80   3. 72
4. 70   5. 81   6. 42

Page 279

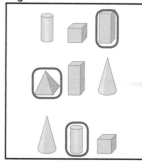

Page 280
Have someone check
your answers.

Page 281

Page 282

Page 283

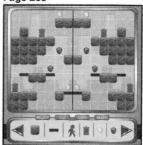

Page 284

Page 285
1. turn   2. flip
3. slide 4. flip

Answers

Page 286
Suggestion:

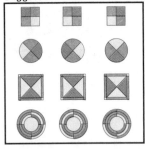

Page 287
1. 5	2. 5	3. 3
4. 11	5. 14	6. 10
7. 7	8. 9	9. 19
10. 9		

Page 288
1. 1, 4, 29   2. 23, 34
3. 6, 16   4. 39, 48
5. 1, 14, 25

Page 289
1. 4, 30   2. 2, 30
3. 2, 0   4. 2, 15
5. 1, 15   6. 1, 0
7. 13, 30

Page 290
1. 3	2. 9	3. 7
4. 10	5. 8	

Page 291
1. 2.45
2. 2.55
3. nacho chips, popcorn
4. granola bar, dried apples
5. 0.45
6. 3.95

Page 292
Suggestion:

Page 293
1. 18.50   2. 6.50
3. 12.50   4. 4.50
5. 20.50   6. 16.50
7. 22.50   8. 10.50
9. 14.50   10. 8.50

Page 294
1. 1	2. 2	3. 9
4. 10	5. 7.50	6. 1.25

Page 295
1. 3	2. 12	3. 3
4. 9	5. likely	6. unlikely

Page 296
1. 35
2. news
3. sitcoms, sports
4. 100
5. 25
6. 155

Page 297
1. 60
2. 80
3. Mandy, Simone
4. Frieda
5. 80
6. 360

Page 298
Have someone check
your answers.

Page 299
1. blue   2. purple
3. 7   4. 20
5. $\frac{1}{2}$ 6. $\frac{1}{4}$

Page 300

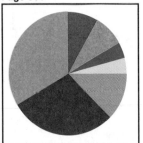

Page 301
1. 2	2. 0	3. 3
4. 5	5. 20	6. 25

Page 302
1. 3
2. 5
3. 6
4. 6
5. May, September, November
6. April

Page 303
1. 1	2. $30
3. $60	4. $80
5. 5	6. likely

Page 304
1. basil	2. lavender
3. 6	4. 7
5. 5	6. lavender

Page 305
Have someone check
your answers.